MEANING AND METHOD IN H. RICHARD NIEBUHR'S THEOLOGY

Douglas F. Ottati

UNIVERSITY
PRESS OF
AMERICA

8210204
Copyright © 1982 by

University Press of America, Inc.

P.O. Box 19101, Washington, D.C. 20036

ISBN (Perfect): 0-8191-2342-0
ISBN   (Cloth): 0-8191-2341-2

The author wishes to thank the following for permission to reprint material:

Harper and Row, Publishers, Inc. for material from The Kingdom of God in America by H. Richard Niebuhr, copyright 1937 by Harper and Row, Publishers, Inc.; from Christ and Culture by H. Richard Niebuhr, copyright 1951 by Harper and Row, Publishers, Inc.; from Radical Monotheism and Western Culture by H. Richard Niebuhr (Harper and Row, 1960), copyright 1943, 1952, 1955, 1960 by H. Richard Niebuhr; from The Responsible Self (Harper and Row, 1963), copyright 1963 by Florence M. Niebuhr.

Macmillan Publishing Co., Inc. for material from The Meaning of Revelation by H. Richard Niebuhr, copyright 1941 by Macmillan Co., Inc., renewed 1969 by Florence Niebuhr, Cynthia Niebuhr, and Richard R. Niebuhr.

Library of Congress Catalog Card Number: 81-43707

For my parents

ACKNOWLEDGEMENTS

This is the text, virtually unrevised, of my doctoral dissertation at the Divinity School of the University of Chicago, submitted in December, 1980. I could not have completed the project without the considerable assistance of my advisory committee, James M. Gustafson, David Tracy, and Larry Greenfield. Langdon Gilkey also read and commented on the earlier drafts. The topic would not have been conceived as it was without the benefit of conversations with Martin Cook and Dennis McCann, who were my fellow students at Chicago.

Thanks are due also to James L. Haney of Concordia College in Minnesota whose reading and counsel improved the early chapters. My colleagues at Union Theological Seminary in Virginia, Donald G. Dawe and John H. Leith have made helpful comments. Richard Dietrich, a student at Union, ably proofread portions of the manuscript. Stephanie D. Patterson and Sally Hicks shared its typing and preparation.

I owe a special debt to my friend, colleague, and teacher, Charles M. Swezey, for countless conversations about H. Richard Niebuhr. The completion of this first scholarly work is an appropriate occasion to acknowledge a special debt to the late Robert F. Evans of the University of Pennsylvania. He was a fine scholar, an able counselor, and a committed churchman.

TABLE OF CONTENTS

ABBREVIATIONS

CAW   H. Richard Niebuhr, Wilhelm Pauck, and
F. P. Miller, The Church Against the World
(Chicago: Willett, Clark and Company, 1935),
156 pp.

CC   H. Richard Niebuhr, Christ and Culture (New
York: Harper and Row, Colophon Books, 1975),
259 pp.

CD   Karl Barth, Church Dogmatics, eds. G. W.
Bromiley and T. F. Torrance, trans. G. W.
Bromiley et al., 4 vols. (Edinburgh: T. and T.
Clark, 1957).

KGA   H. Richard Niebuhr, The Kingdom of God in
America (New York: Harper and Row, Harper
Torchbooks, 1959), 215 pp.

MR   H. Richard Niebuhr, The Meaning of Revelation
(New York: Macmillan Company, Macmillan Paper-
backs, 1960), 144 pp.

RM   H. Richard Niebuhr, Radical Monotheism and
Western Culture with Supplementary Essays (New
York: Harper and Row, Harper Torchbooks, 1970),
144 pp.

RS   H. Richard Niebuhr, The Responsible Self (New
York: Harper and Row, 1963), 183 pp.

SSD   H. Richard Niebuhr, The Social Sources of Denominationalism (New York: World Publishing
Company, A Meridian Book, 1972), 304 pp.

CHAPTER I

INTRODUCTION

Ever since the early Christian communities coined new images and concepts to interpret and communicate the faith, the church has been concerned with the integrity and intelligibility of its message. "Integrity" indicates a concern to communicate the faith in a manner that is true to the distinctive features of the biblical witness. If theology does not correspond to scripture, be it ever so clear and intelligible, it may be doubted whether it communicates anything distinctly Christian. "Intelligibility," on the other hand, signals a concern to present the faith in a manner that is accessible and makes sense to its hearers. If theology does not present the faith in an intelligible manner, be it ever so true to the tradition, one may legitimately doubt whether it really communicates, whether people actually understand it. This double project is one way to define the problem of faith seeking understanding. What the early communities seem to have realized is that theology is preached, and the Christian life is lived, under the pressures of this problem and its requirements.

The use of logos in John 1, for example, meets both criteria. The writer of the Fourth Gospel interprets Christ with the aid of the logos image, but also interprets the logos image through the story of Jesus Christ. Furthermore, the logos image itself has a history in the wisdom literature before John. As a word and concept, therefore, logos forms a bridge or connecting link between the Old Testament, the tradition about Jesus, and Greek thought. It is a part of a language of faith that is true to the historic witness to revelation and at the same time accessible to hearers whose minds and sensibilities have been partly shaped by life in a cultural setting influenced by Greek thought and civilization.

The interpretative situation changes when a portion of the historic witness is solidified or concretized in canonical form. However, one should remain cognizant of the dynamic process by which normative interpretations emerge. In his discussion of law in the Christian life, for example, John Calvin gives priority to scriptural references. But his interpretation is guided also by references to bulwarks of Christian tradition like Augustine, contemporary theologians like Philip Melanchthon, and exponents of natural law like Cicero.[1]

1

The thesis of this dissertation is that the theology of H. Richard Niebuhr adequately resolves the problem of faith seeking understanding in a manner that is at once true to the historically distinctive features of the biblical witness and accessible to its hearers. His constant concern with the relationship of Christ and culture indicates that this problem is near the center of his theology. Niebuhr understood the requirement of integrity and the theological importance of fidelity to the Bible. He knew that faith which can be stated without reference to the irreplaceable images and terms of the biblical witness, like life that can be lived without reference to the values present in the biblical ethos, is not Christian.

On the other hand, Niebuhr also understood that a historic witness bold enough to appropriate the logos concept is unafraid of legitimate interpretation.[2] Indeed, he understood the vitality of this witness theologically as a double movement in Jesus Christ himself from the world to God and from God to the world. He knew further that what constitutes an intelligible statement depends in part on the audience to whom one speaks. With the help of insights drawn from sociology, he described the believer as one who participates at the same time in a cultural matrix and in a Christian community of faith and experience. For Niebuhr, Christians are citizens of a human city who value the accomplishments of their societies and think with the aid of cultural reason as well as citizens of the city of God who remember and are loyal to Jesus Christ. This dual citizenship, in addition to the inherent vitality of the biblical witness, requires that interpretations of Christian faith refer to the wisdom accumulated in culture if they are to be intelligible to their hearers.

The central point can be stated in a more general way. To suppose that theology in the church is essentially the mere repetition of the biblical witness is to proceed on too simple-minded a view of the way both the Bible and the church are imbedded in the societies and cultures in which they are found. Christianity makes use of words, concepts, and knowledge drawn from the culture and everyday language of people. These cultural expressions are used in a religious context which alters and specifies their meaning. Thus, theos does not mean precisely the same thing for the early Christian that it does for the non-Christian Greek in the street, though the apostle Paul believes

2

there are some similarities when he preaches in Athens. Logos does not mean precisely the same thing in early Christian doctrine that it does in the context of Greek philosophy, though Justin Martyr and others believe that there are similarities here as well. Since the faith itself is vital and living, at any given time theology may incorporate language and knowledge which was previously extra-traditional. It is actually untrue to the biblical witness simply to clarify, describe, or repeat it on the assumption that it is static.

Moreover, simply to repeat the biblical witness is to neglect the fact that believers are influenced by their culture and its way of life through participation in general social relations, more formal education, and so on. The language, reason, and values of believers are in large part the language, reason, and values of their culture. For this reason a statement that is intelligible to its hearers in the church needs to engage the everyday cultural language, reason, and values that are communicative currency among believers. An intelligible theology is dynamic and is therefore more accurately characterized as an interpretation of the biblical witness than as a simple repetition of it.

Conversely, to suppose that theological interpretations simply appropriate the common meanings and values of the societies in which the church and scripture are found is to proceed on too simple-minded a view of the way cultural expressions function in Christian tradition and the way language in the church reflects a distinctly Christian sense of the reality of God. As noted above, the placement of words and concepts like theos and logos in the Christian religious context alters and specifies their meaning. This context is governed or regulated by symbols and events which point beyond themselves to a specific perception of divine reality. When theos is used to refer to the one who brought Israel out of Egypt and who is the Father of Jesus Christ, its meaning is altered. When logos is used to refer to the word of God who was in the beginning with God and has been made flesh, its general meaning is altered. When Thomas Aquinas uses the concept of virtue with reference to the Christian life, he does not mean precisely what Aristotle meant by that term. Similarly, when Calvin writes about natural law with reference to the decalogue, its significance is specified in a distinctive way. The statement of a meaning or a value that

3

is true to the tradition needs to include some reference to distinctive symbols, concepts, and events that
are part of the concretized biblical record and which
regulate the significance of ordinary words and knowledge drawn from general culture.

Finally, a purportedly Christian theology
which relies exclusively on general or ordinary terms
neglects the fact that the believer's sense of the
divine reality is embedded in a confession of the
purposes and character of God believed to have been
specially revealed. A theology which overlooks this
fact runs the risk of being unable to distinguish the
specific connotations of words and values within the
Christian context. The meanings of words like logos
and theos in theology as well as the significance of
law and virtue in Christian ethics then remain almost
entirely general and escape explicitly Christian qualification. Thus, a theological interpretation which
elucidates and specifies the believer's sense of
divine reality should include an irreducible reference to the believer's Christian confession.

In sum, a simple repetition of the biblical
witness is not only unintelligible, but also untrue
to scripture. An easy translation of faith into the
idiom of the culture in which the church and scripture
are found not only lacks integrity, but also renders
unintelligible the believer's claim to a distinctive
sense of divine reality. This dual requirement can be
stated in two propositions. Stating the faith intelligibly so that it engages ordinary reason and experience is a requirement for maintaining the integrity of
Christian belief. Stating Christian belief with integrity so that it engages important biblical symbols
and events is a requirement for an intelligible exposition of faith's present experience.

When faith seeking understanding is interpreted in this way, it becomes apparent that Niebuhr
was confronted by theologies which tended to concentrate attention on one or the other pole of the classical Christian project. Karl Barth dramatically articu-
lated a concern for integrity in theology. Yet Barth's
theology failed adequately to connect the meanings and
values of faith with ordinary discourse and experience.
On the other hand, Protestant liberalism exemplified
by Albrecht Ritschl offered an equally dramatic statement of a concern for intelligibility, but often failed
to anchor its interpretation of the faith in an irreducible reference to the biblical witness.3

It would be unfair and untrue to say that liberal theology in the nineteenth century was not concerned with the problem of integrity. Indeed, many liberals consciously regarded their theology as an attempt to recover important elements of the biblical heritage and to interpret the work of the Protestant Reformers. Confronted with the serious challenges of the Enlightenment and modern historiography, however, liberal theologians were understandably occupied with questions of intelligibility. How is Christian theology possible? To what do theological statements refer and how do they have meaning? In certain respects, the bold programs of liberal theology and their historical lives of Jesus may be understood as responses to these questions which sometimes proceeded too uncritically and led to a compromise of Christian truth.[4]

Partly in response to what he considered the excesses and failures of liberal theology, Karl Barth defined dogmatics as the self-examination of the church. For Barth, the question of truth in theology is decided exclusively with reference to God's word in Jesus Christ. In terms of the present discussion, we might say that Barth was appalled at the result of liberal fascination with the problem of intelligibility and so called theology back to the problem of integrity.[5]

One may admit the force and importance of Barth's clarion for recent theology, however, without adopting his position. Taken to its logical conclusion, something Barth did not always do, it is the resounding declaration that theological interpretation need refer only to biblical language and symbols in order to communicate the faith. It implies that the believer need refer his credo to no other standard than Jesus Christ in order to understand the meaning of his faith and talk about God.

Barth's theology short-circuits the project of faith seeking understanding by disallowing connections between biblical images and more ordinary discourse and experience. It frustrates the effort to interpret Christian faith intelligibly. When, for example, Barth asserts the historicity of an event like the resurrection, we expect him to state how this historical claim may be assessed. Instead, however, Barth claims that "the bodily resurrection is a guarantee that it was Jesus who appeared to the disciples and yet insists that no historian can, in the nature of the case, assess this claim."[6] But this is tantamount to saying

5

that ordinary judgments about the historicity of the
resurrection have no bearing on its historicity as an
event for faith. There is no connection between the
biblical language about resurrection and our ordinary
experience of and judgments about historical events.
For the believer who participates in a culture that
takes historical inquiry seriously, it becomes increasingly difficult to specify the sense in which
Barth asks us to believe that the resurrection is
historical.[7]

        Barth's dogmatic method also requires that
Christian life be governed by unique divine utterances.
Since he believes that God's freedom to speak and his
sovereignty to command are threatened by generalizations about the significance of faith for moral life,
Barth counsels the believer to listen for the word of
God in the moment.[8] Again, however, it becomes difficult to specify how moral directives obtained in this
way may be critically assessed. Can the Christian
legislator explain his policy decisions by referring
exclusively and directly to a unique word of God pri-
vately discernible to persons of Christian faith and
still discharge his responsibility to account for his
actions publicly? Can the medical doctor who is a
Christian responsibly explain his moral decisions to
others exclusively on the basis of an appeal to divine
utterances discernible to Christians alone, or does he
have a moral obligation to explain how his decisions
account for the values that his companions in culture
share?

        Though it would be unfair to say that neo-
orthodoxy was untroubled by questions of intelligibility, Barth's insistence on the uniqueness of theological discourse is typical of many neo-orthodox theologians.[9] By contrast, liberal theology in America
tended to concentrate its effort on the problem of intelligibility or the relevance of Christian faith for
social life. At Harvard, Francis Peabody wrote about
the importance of Jesus for the contemporary "social
question." At Chicago, Shailer Matthews tried to interpret the relevance of Jesus's teaching on social
institutions through the emerging discipline of social
psychology.

        Walter Rauschenbusch expressed a common con-
cern of American liberals in A Theology for the Social
Gospel. "If theology stops growing," he wrote, "or is
unable to adjust itself to its modern environment and
to meet its present, it will die."[10] Like Peabody and

others, Rauschenbusch found scripture and a sensitivity to moral dimensions of modern social questions mutually illuminating. He emphasized that modern society is characterized by a wide social and institutional matrix of interdependence. Relying on what he called the "ethical monotheism" of Jesus and the prophets, he found that the biblical witness also emphasized the importance of social solidarity in the symbol of God's kingdom.

For Rauschenbusch, sin is the antithesis of social solidarity, the "conflict between the selfish Ego and the common good of humanity; or, expressing it in religious terms . . . the conflict between self and God."[11] The kingdom of God is the resolution of this conflict. Moreover, since the common good may be defined by a correct understanding of the social situation, the meaning of God's kingdom can be translated into a contemporary conceptuality.

On this interpretation, the ethical relevance of the kingdom can be discussed without fear of contradiction, since moral issues can be addressed in light of a public conception of the common good. Yet one may legitimately question whether much that is specifically Christian is not finally compromised rather than conveyed by this procedure. Surely, Rauschenbusch is right to say that the biblical witness contains a genuine concern for social justice. But the biblical symbol of the kingdom refers not only to God's will for a moral order; it also refers to his eschatological action which enters like a thief in the night without deference to the moral strivings of men. In his devotion to the kingdom, Jesus seems not only the bearer of moral ideals but also the advocate and example of a radically religious devotion to God who looks forward to his eschatological action. When God's kingdom is too closely or easily identified with contemporary understandings of the common good, it becomes possible to define the telos of the Christian life almost exclusively with reference to cultural interpretations of morality.[12]

One should not neglect the persuasiveness with which Rauschenbusch addressed many social issues. Nevertheless, doubts about the adequacy of his theology are increased by the fact that the marks of Christian life and the church seem reducible to general ethical criteria. This alternative appears to identify the true Christian and the true church with that segment of culture which fulfills the moral requirement of sincere social involvement in solidarity with others to bring about the common good. Thus, it reflects a culture-Christianity which threatens to eliminate important elements of the tradition.

On the basis of these observations, it follows that an intelligible theology needs to refer to cultural reasoning about human experience and the world in order to state the relevance of faith to all areas of life. When, in the course of this task, theology makes claims which impinge on accepted areas of inquiry, the theologian should indicate how these claims are open to investigation by the area of inquiry in question. To the extent that theology makes cognitive claims which impinge on the fields of history or the social sciences, for example, it should also indicate how these claims are open to critical investigation. Similarly, to the extent that theology makes moral claims, it should also indicate how they may be assessed by the discipline of ethics. An intelligible theology cannot enjoy the benefits of these claims without also accepting their risks. If this is not recognized, the believer who participates in a culture that ordinarily makes these critical judgments will be confused, and perhaps even led to question whether faith itself is an irresponsible act.

The primary concern of a theology which follows these general guidelines is not to commend the faith to non-believers, though non-believers may find an intelligible theology engaging. Rather, the methodological procedures outlined here have their principal value insofar as they aid the believer in the continuing project of bringing Christian faith to bear on all aspects of life. It is when this project of a confessing, committed, and reasoning faith is thwarted that the believer is likely to be confused and deterred from making sense of his or her Christian life.

On the other hand, a theology that adequately addresses the problem of integrity needs to maintain a prominent reference to the biblical witness in order to uphold the distinctiveness of faith's sense of divine reality. A theology that is true to this witness cannot offer an uncritical or complete translation of traditional terms and symbols into the ordinary language of culture without compromising the integrity of Christian faith and life. There is a dimension that does not easily fit the mold of ordinary discourse. Thus, the kingdom of God cannot be reduced to cultural interpretations of morality without

8

neglecting the sense in which it refers to a distinct action of God.

When the claims of faith impinge upon accepted methods of inquiry, a theology concerned for integrity resists the uncritical reduction of religious claims. When, for example, faith claims that God led Israel out of Egypt, this statement includes and depends on a historical judgment. But the religious claim cannot be collapsed into the historical claim. The two are not equivalent. Similarly, if faith makes ethical claims in connection with the kingdom of God, theology should recognize that the biblical symbol is not reducible to its ethical dimension.

It is now apparent that the construction of a theology which is true to the distinctive features of the biblical witness and accessible to its hearers requires at least the outlines of a comprehensive position. One needs to articulate an understanding of the content to be communicated as well as the principles of method which facilitate communication. For this reason, our thesis needs to be set in the context of a wider interpretative argument. A theology that is at once true to the historically distinctive features of the biblical witness and accessible to its hearers emerges in Niebuhr's writings because he develops a distinct alternative to liberal theology on the one hand and to crisis theology on the other.

In many respects, this alternative is an attempt to combine the seemingly contradictory emphases which characterize theologians like Barth and Rauschenbusch. As we trace the emergence of this position in Niebuhr's writings, it will be possible to develop criteria for integrity and intelligibility. For example, the compatibility of appeals to special revelatory experiences in theology with general interpretations of human knowing is important for Niebuhr's theory of revelation. Unlike Karl Barth, Niebuhr is concerned to show how appeals to revelation are compatible with historical relativity as well as belief in divine sovereignty. This suggests that the coherence of major appeals in theology with some general and consistent philosophical principles is one criterion for an intelligible theology.

Niebuhr's theory of revelation indicates how theological claims about the meaning and significance of historical events may be distinct from yet compatible with the claims of critical historiography. Also, his development of the metaphor of responsibility takes account of contemporary philosophical and scientific knowledge about human behavior. This suggests that an intelligible theology should indicate how its claims are open to critical assessment from the perspectives of other inquiries while, at the same time, it maintains integrity by insisting that theological interpretations are not reducible to the terms of other inquiries.

Finally, belief in the sovereign Lord of nature and history requires theology to strive toward a comprehensive vision of all things related to God. Some of Niebuhr's shorter articles, his interpretation of western culture, and his Christian moral philosophy are steps toward a comprehensive interpretation of human experience in light of Christian faith. Though the finality of this vision is qualified by historical conditioning and the effects of sin, it suggests that an adequate theology will sketch a comprehensive view of human existence which has integrity in light of the biblical ethos and intelligibility in light of contemporary knowledge.

If preoccupations with one or the other pole of faith seeking understanding characterize many theologians with whom Niebuhr was in dialogue, similarly inadequate proposals remain influential. Some contemporary theologians, like Paul Holmer, construct interpretations of Christian faith which isolate the meaning of theological doctrines from our present, non-theological knowledge about human existence and the world.[13] These theologies may be read as attempts to guard the integrity of Christian faith and may even be said to show its relevance to some aspects of ordinary life. But they lead to interpretations of doctrine which believers necessarily find confusing and, therefore, represent deficient responses to the problem of intelligibility.

Other contemporaries offer less than adequate responses to the problem of integrity. Schubert Ogden, for example, interprets Christian faith in such a way that it "re-presents" the essential self-understanding of modern people.[14] While interpretations of this sort display the relevance of important aspects of Christian faith, they tend to translate its distinctive symbols into the conceptual idioms of contemporary philosophies too easily.

I am persuaded that a central tradition in

Christian theology, which includes Augustine, Calvin, Wesley, and Edwards has historically urged believers to participate responsibly in culture without becoming identical with it. Neither the untimely rejection of cultural reasoning nor the timely translation of Christian faith into cultural terms is compatible with this classical interpretation. This does not mean that other positions are ultimately either false or non-Christian. In fact, some have argued that Christians in the modern world must choose between a life curiously out of step with the times and a life in complete harmony with the dominant values of their culture. It does mean, however, that inadequate resolutions of the problem of faith seeking understanding are discontinuous with important aspects of Christian faith and life as this classical tradition has understood them. Theologians ought at least to be aware of the serious turn of events.

I have tried to indicate Niebuhr's agreements and differences with the more extreme proposals of crisis and liberal theologians in the text that follows. This is particularly true of the first three chapters, which discuss his decisive break with the approach of the Social Gospel, his concern for divine sovereignty and the subjective experience of faith, and his theory of revelation. For Niebuhr, the objective perception of the sovereign God requires a transformation of human values and experience rather than their uncritical support or negation.

The fourth chapter shows how Christ and Culture clarifies this transformationist stance in relation to other normative theological positions. It also clarifies the sense in which other proposals are discontinuous with this transformationist tradition in Christian thought. The fifth chapter analyzes Radical Monotheism and The Responsible Self as attempts to reinterpret human experience in light of Christian faith. In the conclusion, I have tried to sketch constructive implications of Niebuhr's theology in a systematic fashion and to bring it into dialogue with the contemporary alternatives posed by Holmer and Ogden.

Notes

[1]John Calvin, The Institutes of the Christian Religion, ed. John T. McNeill, trans. Ford Lewis Battles, The Library of Christian Classics, vols. 20 and 21 (Philadelphia: The Westminster Press, 1960), 20:348-362; 21:1052-1053.

[2]Niebuhr believes that the writer of the Fourth Gospel "undertakes not only to translate the gospel of Jesus Christ into the concepts of Hellenistic readers, but also lifts these ideas about Logos and knowledge, truth and eternity, to new levels of meaning by interpreting them through Christ." See CC, pp. 196-197. Elsewhere he notes that Paul used Greek language, habits of life and thought-forms "to make the good news of salvation intelligible to the citizens of another world," that Calvin formulated the third use of the law to express the new life of grace in culture, and that Augustine and Aquinas appropriately used Platonic and Aristotelian philosophies as tools by means of which to express a truth beyond philosophy. See "The Christian Evangel and Social Cultures," Religion in Life 8 (January 1939): 44-48.
In 1960, Niebuhr called for "a resymbolization of the message and the life of faith in the One God" like those which accompanied the Reformation, the Puritan movement, the Great Awakening, the deeds of the Franciscans and the social gospelers. Both the present experience of a living faith and continuity with the past are prerequisites for this resymbolization. Our old phrases will not do. But resymbolization is not possible "unless one has direct relations in the immediacy of personal life to the actualities to which people in another time referred with the aid" of now traditional symbols. See "Reformation: Continuing Imperative," The Christian Century 77 (March 1960): 251.

[3]According to Niebuhr, Ritschl correctly identified the relation between man and God as a value-relation. But Ritschl also posits a prior value-relation, namely, man in opposition to nature. MR, p. 24. Problems of integrity arise when Ritschl approaches God from the standpoint of this prior value-relation. In this context, God becomes the One who supports the human spirit in its struggle, and Christianity may be described as "the perfect moral religion" because it presents the kingdom of God as a community of spirit that rises above the natural limits of history. See Albrecht Ritschl, The Christian Doctrine of Justification and Reconciliation, eds. H. R. Mackintosh and

A. B. Macaulay, trans. A. B. Macaulay (Clifton, New Jersey: Reference Book Publishers, 1966), p. 10. Indeed, Ritschl could claim that the kingdom of God is the highest good of those united in it "to the degree that it offers the solution to the question propounded or implied in all religions: How can man, recognizing himself as part of the world and at the same time capable of spiritual personality, attain to that dominion over the world, as opposed to limitation by it, which this capability gives him the right to claim?" See Albrecht Ritschl, Three Essays, trans. Philip Hefner (Philadelphia: Fortress Press, 1972), p. 224.

This feature of Ritschl's theology tends to visualize God siding with one part of his creation against another. It seems inconsistent with the biblical affirmation of God as the Creator and Governor of nature and history. It also opens the door for judging the value of Christian faith by an alien standard, namely, its utility in enabling the human spirit to obtain the ultimate victory over nature. Moreover, it now becomes possible to describe God and humanity as co-workers bringing about a common goal, and even to describe the kingdom as the ultimate goal of culture's best efforts without explicit reference to God. This enables one to talk about the value of Christian faith in public terms, but it runs counter to the biblical affirmation of divine sovereignty.

Niebuhr's criticism is that Ritschl began to talk about God from a viewpoint other than the viewpoint of Christian faith. This opened the door for certain aberrations in theology, though Ritschl cannot be blamed for all the consequences which have followed.

[4]Schubert M. Ogden, The Reality of God (New York: Harper and Row, Paperback Edition, 1977), p. 4.

[5]CD, 1/1: 3, 4, 6, 12-13, 18-21, 29, 31-32, 82. For Barth, liberal understandings of the relation between faith and theology as well as more recent existentialist ones represent the continuation of the pietist tradition and the "anthropologizing" of theology. Jesus Christ is the "being of the Church" and the true criterion for dogmatics which must be distinguished from all other standards. It is an egregious error to judge theological utterances by alien criteria, like those of historians and philosophers. Getting the message straight or avoiding heresy is the primary concern of theology. "At every point . . . dogmatics is a struggle between the reason of man and the revelation believed in the Church." A basic task of dogmatics is to test the orthodoxy of preaching in the

present age. "The problem of dogmatics is that of the purity of doctrine, or the problem of the Word of God in Christian proclamation." CD, 1/2: 792.

[6]Van A. Harvey, The Historian and the Believer (New York: Macmillan Co., 1966), p. 157.

[7]The historical question emerges at a number of points in Barth's theology. It is present, though not central, in his discussion of the virgin birth, which he regards chiefly as a sign of the mystery of revelation and incarnation. CD, 1/2: 172-202. Barth notes that "there is certainly nothing to prevent anyone, without affirming the doctrine of the Virgin Birth, from recognizing the mystery of the person of Jesus Christ or from believing in a perfectly Christian way." Nevertheless, "this does not imply that the Church is at liberty to convert the doctrine of the Virgin Birth into an option for specially strong or specially weak souls." CD, 1/2: 181. He then claims that the miracle is "an event occurring in the realm of the creaturely world in the full sense of the word, and so in the unity of the psychical with the physical, in time and space, in noetic and ontic reality. It cannot be understood out of continuity with the rest that occurs in this world, nor is it in fact grounded in this continuity." CD, 1/2: 181.
One may admire Barth's insistence on the theological significance of the virgin birth as well as his refusal to equate its theological import with its historicity, and still wonder exactly what kind of historical claim he intends. He seems to say that the virgin birth cannot be understood out of continuity with other historical events and yet that it cannot be understood in continuity with them either. At the very least, one must conclude that Barth does not clearly indicate what the faithful are to believe about the virgin birth as an historical event. Perhaps this ambiguity is a specific implication of his earlier insistence that it is inappropriate to judge "the utterances of the Church about God" by the alien principles of sciences like history. CD, 1/1: 6.
The same question emerges with final seriousness in Barth's discussion of the resurrection and the Easter appearances. He says that this is the "key to the whole" gospel and that "we are here in the sphere of history and time no less than in the case of the words and acts and even the death of Jesus." CD, 3/2: 442-443. He also claims that anything other than the affirmation of a literal, bodily and physical resurrection falls "into Docetism at the crucial point." CD,

14

3/2: 448. Affirmation of a physical bodily resurrection is important because it is the seal of continuity between the earthly and risen Lord, and because it is crucial that the center of the "history" of Jesus Christ include "nature." CD, 3/2: 448, 451.

At the same time, however, Barth maintains that the New Testament narratives "are describing an event beyond the reach of historical research or depiction." CD, 3/2: 452. For our purposes, it is not necessary to review Barth's extended critique of Bultmann's assumptions about history, or to show that Barth's rather monolithic view of historical judgment and reconstruction is inadequate. Van Harvey has already argued that views of historiography as a single method and set of assumptions are naive. See Harvey, The Historian and the Believer, pp. 38-102. Our point is less complex. Barth appears to claim that the resurrection is an historical event with all of the characteristics of ordinary historical events. At the same time, he claims that resurrection, in the nature of the case, can never be subject to critical historical scrutiny. Moreover, "we have no right to try to analyse or harmonize" the New Testament stories of the resurrection and the appearances. CD, 3/2: 452.

If this is so, how are the faithful to have any clear idea of what they are being asked to believe about the resurrection as the "key to the whole" gospel? Barth seems more concerned to defend affirmations that he believes are theologically essential and true to the New Testament record than to show how these affirmations are intelligible to believers who think with the aid of their cultural reason and experience.

[8]When Barth speaks of "complete openness" to the command of God as the norm of moral actions, he means openness to a norm that cannot be formulated as a general rule, one that is "new every morning," and without parallel in non-Christian ethical theories. CD, 2/2: 645-647. The divine command is given its full concreteness in the present. It needs no interpretation. We cannot account for its validity as a moral norm by any human standard that is generally available. CD, 2/2: 661-664, 669-671. Divine commands are therefore clearly beyond the pale of public discussions of human responsibility and accountability, since such discussions presuppose some more or less definite common standards.

Barth modifies his position in CD, 3/4: 3-46, where he speaks of spheres or orders of divine action and of a definite structure of human moral responsibility that parallels prominent lines of divine action

15

within these spheres or orders. This introduces more
regularity in Christian moral life than his earlier
discussion implies, and it also qualifies the tendency
toward situationalism in the earlier volume. But it
does not change Barth's position with regard to public
accountability, since he dissociates the divine orders
from all natural or non-theological knowledge. See CD,
3/4: 45.

[9]Ogden, The Reality of God, p. 15.

[10]Walter Rauschenbusch, A Theology for the Social
Gospel (Nashville: Abingdon Press, 1945), p. 1.

[11]Ibid., pp. 46-47.

[12] For Rauschenbusch, the Social Gospel minimizes
non-ethical religious practices and beliefs. See
ibid., pp. 14-15.

[13]For Holmer, theology interprets the passions of
the human heart in light of the abiding verities of God
contained in scripture. But theological interpretation
of these abiding verties in scripture is entirely independent from historical interpretation of scripture.
And, theological interpretation of the passions of the
heart is entirely independent of knowledge about human
existence and the world obtained from other quarters,
e.g. social science. Thus, what is true of scripture
theologically has no relation to what is true about
scripture in non-theological terms, and what is true
of the passions of the human heart theologically has
no relation to what is true about human existence and
the world in non-theological terms. But this is tantamount to a doctrine of double or even multiple truth
from which the believer is not likely to soon recover.
For example, though Holmer eschews specific examples,
what does it mean to say that the resurrection of Jesus
Christ is theologically true on these grounds? See
Paul L. Holmer, The Grammar of Faith (New York: Harper
and Row, 1978), pp. 5-6, 12-15, 69, 78, 79-80.

[14]A detailed examination of Ogden's position appears in chapter six. Here I only note that, for
Ogden, the primary characteristic of modern people and
their self-understanding is the affirmation that autonomous, secular life is ultimately meaningful and worthwhile. Ogden argues that this confidence is implicitly
and inevitably theistic. "It is [God's] own creative
becoming that is the ultimate cause advanced or re-
tarded by all our lesser causes and their issues."

This is the same theistic faith "decisively represented" in Jesus Christ. Jesus Christ represents
a faith in God that is basic to autonomous life and
its self-understanding. The question of integrity
here is whether this understanding of autonomous human
life and the corollary of persuasive divine activity,
which is quite consistent with Process philosophy, is
adequate to biblical portraits of judgment and eschatology as well as the human responses to these divine
actions. See The Reality of God, pp. 64, 65, 70, 125,
142.

CHAPTER II

THE ETHICAL PROBLEM OF THE CHURCH

The Social Sources of Denominationalism reflects Niebuhr's enduring concerns with the relation
between the gospel and culture and the relation between
faith and ethics.[1] This combination of interests comes
to expression in a social and historical analysis of
American Christianity for at least three reasons. From
Ernst Troeltsch and Max Weber, Niebuhr learned that a
historical entity can be understood in its concrete
relations with other cultural factors only through historical method and analysis. Like any other set of
institutions, then, Christian churches have important
social and historical dimensions which the moral theologian ignores at his peril.

Second, Troeltsch's The Social Teaching of the
Christian Churches taught Niebuhr that Christianity's
location in culture makes adaptation to the conditions
of civilization inevitable.[2] The integrity of the gospel is subject to compromise and even sacrifice in the
interest of cultural values and practices. For Niebuhr,
the religious communities and institutions that emerge
from this process closely follow "the division of men
into castes of national, racial, and economic groups."[3]
Doctrinal explanations of their divisions are, therefore, inadequate.[4] The churches are social organizations whose principle of differentiation needs to be
sought in their conformity to the order of social
classes and interests.[5]

Finally, Niebuhr is driven to historical and
sociological analysis by what he calls "the evil of denominationalism," the apparent failure of the American
churches to transcend social conditions and to resist
making self-preservation "the primary object of their
endeavor."[6] His main thesis is that denominationalism
is an unacknowledged hypocrisy.[7] Christians have seen
to it that their racial and class loyalties are not
jeopardized by an unswerving loyalty to the gospel.
Before a resolution to the ethical problem of denominationalism can be put forth, the concrete dimensions of
its apostasy must be grasped and understood. Before
the church can overcome fatal divisions, it must learn
to acknowledge the sinful character of its organization.

In this respect, Niebuhr's analysis functions
as an exposé. The ideal of unity that is implicit in
Jesus' teaching and explicit in Paul's theology throws

19

the sinful divisiveness of the churches into sharp re-
lief.[8] Niebuhr uses history in light of this theological ideal to reveal sin. Social analysis shows that
American Christianity is in danger of losing its integrity as an emissary of the gospel ideal, and loss
of integrity results in the ethical and social irrel-
evance of the church. The denominations have failed
to show "that faith makes a difference in the individual and in the social life."[9] Rather than offer an
alternative to divisive, self-interested standards in
culture, the denominations have been co-opted by them.

For Niebuhr, denominational Christianity in
America must be examined from the perspective of social
science, not only because any organization has obvious
historical and social dimensions, but also because it
has capitulated to self-interested cultural ideals.
The ethical problem of the church lies in its inability
to distinguish legitimate adaptation to a cultural environment from the adoption of non-Christian values.[10]

In light of the ideal of organic solidarity,
Niebuhr chronicles the divisions in the church which
result from dependence on self-interested social influences. The American Civil War and the emancipation of slaves become occasions for regional and
racial schism.[11] The immigration of foreign nationals
to the American "melting pot" occasions still further
divisions.[12]

After nine chapters of scathing criticism,
Niebuhr urges the church to return to the gospel ideal
of unity as one which is able to command a deeper, more
extensive loyalty than self-interested denominational
standards.[13] His guiding vision is plain. Ever since
New Testament times, the church has fallen from its
original unity.[14] There is a fundamental disjunction
between the ethical ideal of Christianity and its
social reality.

The obvious criticism of Niebuhr's final appeal
is that it fails to get at the root of the problem. If
Christians have fallen away from their unitary ideal
due to the influences of persistent social factors,
why should a simple call for repristination bring them
back? Moreover, his characterizations of the kingdom
are couched in the language of liberal humanism and
succumb to the cultural co-optation they seek to replace. He describes the kingdom as "the ideal of
brotherhood," the "harmony of love," and the "fellowship of love," while he notes the importance of human

solidarity.[15] But each of these expressions suggests
that the kingdom ideal can function independently of
an explicit reference to God. They indicate that
Niebuhr views the ethical problem of the church as
the difficulty of obtaining a quasi-religious synthesis that will integrate the interests of nations
and classes into a harmonious society.[16]

This ideal leads one commentator to say that
Niebuhr seems dissatisfied with the final chapter even
as he writes it.[17] Niebuhr himself records dissatis-
faction with this "new appeal to good will" eight years
later.[18] Precisely because of its shortcomings, however, the final appeal in Social Sources helps to illumine Niebuhr's later work.

The statement that religion provides civilization with a synthesis built on a common world-view and
a common ethics indicates a particular understanding
of integrity and intelligibility. From this perspective, the problem with the church is its failure to be
selective, to support the tendencies in culture toward
social solidarity which accord with the gospel ideal.
Demands for integrity and intelligibility converge,
since republication of the theological ideal provides
the church with the appropriate biblical criterion for
selection as well as the key to an ethical synthesis
for the modern world. In fact, the ideal of fellowship
is "the hope of Christendom and the world" which challenges "the world to recall its better nature."[19]

From this perspective, integrity requires that
one construct a vision of the ethical ideal which is
true to the biblical portraits. An ideal commonwealth
that duplicates the essential unitary features of the
kingdom is the standard by which one evaluates the
social reality of the church and its cultural environment. Intelligibility is the task of describing the
ideal so that it synthesizes the highest social and
moral aspirations of western culture. Once this has
been done, the relevance of the church's ideal is assured, since it criticizes society's less worthy interests in light of culture's highest ethical goal.

There are at least three difficulties with this
proposal when measured by Niebuhr's mature transformationist stance in Christ and Culture. First, it tends
to collapse faith in God into a cultural loyalty to
human fellowship. At times, it seems possible to
equate Christian faith in the kingdom with loyalty to
the ideal of a unified civilization. Second, Niebuhr's

21

exhortation presupposes a deficient doctrine of sin.
His "new appeal to good will" assumes that sin does not
radically infect the wellspring of human action, that
our wills are healthy and able to pursue effectively
the true good if only we are reminded of what it is.
Given this assumption, a basic reorientation of human
personality by God's converting influences is unneces-
sary. Grace does not transform nature, but selectively
supports humanity's best established tendencies. It,
therefore, seems possible to describe Christian moral
life apart from any explicit reference to the reality
of God and the workings of divine grace.

Belieful Realism

During the years from 1930 to 1935, Niebuhr
comes to enduring convictions about the sense of moral
obligation which accompanies Christian faith, the
radical nature of sin, and the sovereignty of God.[20]
His brother Reinhold reports that Richard is now at
work on the problem of "dissociating a rigorous gospel
ethic of disinterestedness from the sentimental dilu-
tions of that ethic which are current in liberal
Christianity."[21] The discovery which forms the context for these emerging convictions is a different
understanding of faith in God called belieful realism.

After Social Sources, Niebuhr becomes increasingly concerned with the difficulty of affirming a
Christian ethic in the modern world. Moral relativism,
which he calls the disintegrating "acid of modernity,"
simply presents competing ethical systems without shed-
ding light on how one may legitimately affirm a specific
moral value.[22] The result is a crisis of moral authority. The Christian ethic appears as one system of
morality among many, and is in danger of disappearing
in a tangled forest of moral values.

In shorter articles, Niebuhr sharpens his effort to present the Christian ethic "apart from its
unholy alliance with civilization" by distinguishing
its basic commitment from the dominant interests of
culture.[23] Christianity, he writes, is as homeless in
the capitalistic and communistic societies of the modern world "as it was in the Roman empire which perse-
cuted it and in the medieval feudalism which patronized
it." The great temptation of faith is to find "a rest-
ing place for its homelessness."[24] In its excessive
optimism, the social gospel has failed to take the
facts of evil and divine sovereignty seriously.[25] A
frank recognition of human sinfulness and dependence

22

on God leads to different strategies in a Christian
approach to practical life in the world.[26]

The initial step in Niebuhr's effort to identify a distinctive Christian ethic is to gain a clear
view of its religious foundation. In "Religion and
Ethics," he maintains that faith and ethics are insep-
arable and indivisible, but that they cannot be simply
identified.[27] The sense of obligation necessary for
the affirmation of a moral value is a feature of religious devotion to ultimate reality. But the simple
identification of religion and ethics supports a tendency to view religion in purely social terms as an aid
to morality.[28] On the other hand, the complete separation of faith from moral values leads to a "religion
within the limits of deity" that has few identifiable
moral consequences.[29] If the former leads to an ethics
inconsistent with Christian faith, the latter "becomes
a theology without content; it stops where it begins--
with the assertion of divine transcendence."[30]

Niebuhr concludes that "the peril of ethics
alone is relativity, and the peril of isolated religion
is the unintelligible dogmatism of an absolute, irrel-
evant to time."[31] The older liberal theology tends to
equate faith with devotion to a moral value and thereby
threatens the irreducible reference of faith to God.
The newer crisis theology threatens the moral relevance
of faith by asserting that there is no connection between faith in God and ordinary moral experience.[32]

These concerns lead Niebuhr into the ranks of
a broad movement called "religious realism," a revolt
against modern humanism's glorification of human nature.[33] For many astute minds cruelly shaken by war
and world-wide depression, realism means a break with
the nineteenth century conviction that man is the
measure of all things. In philosophy, it means a
turn from the perceiving subject toward the object of
perception pioneered by thinkers like Husserl and
Heidegger. For theology, according to Douglas Clyde
Macintosh, it means the view that a religious object
exists independently of human consciousness and yet
that we may obtain practically valuable knowledge of
its nature from our experience.[34]

Niebuhr himself understands realism in art,
philosophy, and religion as a testimony to reality's
stubborn independence from the eye of the beholder. In
"Religious Realism in the Twentieth Century," he writes
that the nineteenth century successfully restored the

human mind to the center of the cosmos. This restoration ends with critical naturalism and pragmatism which regard the world as a mental construct if not simply a useful mental fiction.35   In religion the temper of liberalism issues, as we have seen, in the moralization of faith. Faith becomes subject-centered and is valued as an aid in the struggle for the human good rather than as a human relation to transcendent reality.   "The final fruit of this development is modern humanism with its elimination from religion of all but human objects and purposes." 36

        The theology of crisis represents a crucial protest against this anthropocentric domestication of faith in God. To Niebuhr, the beginnings of realism in theology are discernible in the assertion and defense of religious faith as a distinct experience after nineteenth century efforts to reduce it to morality failed.37   Troeltsch's concern with the philosophy of religion, his many-sided fight against reductionism, and Otto's concern with the idea of the holy are the beginnings of a new direction. But the movement becomes definite when it turns from the subjective experience of faith to its objective content. Barth's blistering realism is an "effort to define revelation in wholly nonpsychological terms" and to distinguish the reality of God from all ordinary experiences and ideas. 38

        For Niebuhr, however, Barth and the crisis theologians have turned toward the religious object at the expense of any enduring relation between God and human life. They have banished questions of how people apprehend God and what consequence this apprehension has for human living in favor of a dogmatic assertion that God is independently and transcendently real. The cost is too dear.

        If the nineteenth century, beginning with
        the subject, could discover no way that leads
        from subject to object, from man to God, then
        this twentieth century theology beginning with
        the object fails to find a way to the subject,
        from God to man. 39

In either case, theology fails to understand faith as a relation between the transcendent and the mundane apprehended in human experience.

        Influenced by Paul Tillich, Niebuhr begins to develop an alternative understanding of faith during the early thirties. For Tillich, belieful realism points to an essentially religious dimension implicit in human life.[40] Beneath the cleavage between theory and practice, there is a "faithful" attitude toward ultimate reality.[41] This basic apprehension of transcendent reality remains independent of our theoretical and practical ideas, though it penetrates all aspects of human behavior. Thus, while faith in God cannot be simply equated with our speculative doctrines and moral ideals, neither can it be irretrievably divorced from our ordinary experience. Speculative ideas, artistic creations, and practical actions are expressions of this prior faith.

For the Christian theologian, the transcendent reference implicit in human life is made explicit by Christian belief in God.[42] Christian believing becomes the touchstone, the critical standard by which the diverse expressions of human faith may be assessed. From this perspective, symbols and ideas are idolatrous when they express a faith directed toward lesser objects and thwart the reference of life to truly transcendent reality.[43] So also, our affirmations of moral values and our patterns of practical life are pernicious when they express and abet faith in less than ultimate reality.

The importance of this discovery is difficult to overemphasize. Like a religious symbol, the morphology or skein of one's practical life expresses an implicit faith. Thus, different patterns of moral life reflect different faith commitments which are open to analysis. This is the deep connection between faith and ethics, and it is the task of the moral theologian to make it explicit.

A sermonic essay entitled "What Then Must We Do?" reflects Niebuhr's new position. Confronted with a pervasive loss of meaning in the midst of economic depression, the preacher's first line of attack is to view the present disorder as the consequence of sin. Our query, says Niebuhr, is no longer "the question of builders of the kingdom of God on earth but the question of Cain" raised by a sick world. [44]

In our dealing with ourselves and with our neighbors, with our societies and our neighbor societies, we deal not with morally and rationally healthy beings, who may be called upon to develop ideal personalities and to build ideal commonwealths, but rather with diseased beings, who can do little or nothing until they have recovered health.[45]

A true apprehension of human sin leads to the judgment that the basic commitments and devotions of the human personality are ill and in need of a physician. This is the fundamental malaise which the preacher-theologian must address, and it is a corruption deeper than our moral ideals. The moral question "What shall we do?" refers beyond itself to the objects of human faith, hope, and trust. In light of the explicit reference of Christian faith to God, theology unmasks false loyalties. Surrounded by failed economic and political institutions, we cannot realistically hope that yet another human work or invention will remedy our ultimate problem. We must, says Niebuhr, divest ourselves of our idols.

Once our idolatry has been unmasked and the appropriate faith-context for moral life has been distinguished, it is possible to identify a pattern for moral life that expresses loyalty to the truly transcendent God. Christ's teaching and example offer such a pattern; one not as stirring, perhaps as the delusion of another utopian ideal, but one that insists on the reference of daily living to divine reality and one which exhorts us to repent. Through Christ, says Niebuhr, we recognize love, sacrifice, and sharing as the order of reality which "we have flouted too long" in our loyalty to ourselves and our societies. [46]

One may question whether an article like this one pays sufficient attention to political and economic factors which contribute to the concrete situation. But the focus of the essay, as of so many of Niebuhr's writings, is not casuistry but moral theology. Its purpose is to show that the ethical question "What shall we do?" touches finally on the question of loyalty, the question of faith's valued object or the god in whom people trust and with reference to which their lives have form and meaning. Indeed, it is not too much to say that the moral question leads finally to the question of the New Testament, "What must we do to be saved?"

At precisely this point, moral theology tries to make plain the dependence of human life on God. One's dominant loyalty or faith is a prime factor contributing to the orientation of moral life.[47] Sin is essentially idolatry, a perversion or misdirection of human faith toward objects that are less than ultimate,

26

and which issues in a pattern of practical life that is
out of kilter with the order of reality. But both the
objective order of love, sacrifice, and sharing and the
reorientation of human faith depend on factors largely
beyond our control. Divine sovereignty means that
human life is dependent on God's activity reflected in
the order of reality and that nothing less than God's
reconciling action can restore an appropriate orientation to human life.

In The Church Against the World, Niebuhr recasts the ethical problem of the church from this perspective. The church is no longer the vehicle for a
cultural synthesis of moral ideals. Moral standards of
civilization are important, but they are not necessarily the standards of the church. As an individual may
profit from the criticism of others and yet recognize
that they judge him by standards that are not his own,
so the church is under no obligation to conform to the
world's principles.

Seen from the inside, the question of the
church is not how it can live up to society's expectations or what it must do to save civilization, but
rather how it can be true to itself.[48] From the
church's viewpoint, the threat against it is made not
by a turbulent world, but by the transcendent God.
The church directs its question to "its sovereign
Lord." What must it do to be saved?[49]

In phrases reminiscent of Social Sources,
Niebuhr asserts that the church is imperiled by compromise.[50] But unlike Social Sources, here the worldliness
which has infiltrated the church is analyzed theologically as idolatry: the perversion of the true reference
of life to that which gives meaning. Idolatry is the
worship of images rather than that which they image.[51]

> It appears whenever finite and relative
> things or powers are regarded as ends-in-
> themselves, where civilization is valued
> for civilization's sake, where life is
> lived for life's sake, or nation adored
> for nation's sake.[52]

As the prime expression of sin, idolatry mistakenly
ascribes absolute worth to a finite thing or symbol
which is meant to point beyond itself. It frustrates
the relation between human life and transcendent reality. For Niebuhr, then, worldliness is a false perversion of true faith. It is faith in self rather than

the faith of a self in the transcendent object that
gives meaning to selfhood. [53]

One consequence of sin is conflict between self
and society. If the loyalties of persons and groups
are not trained upon the one God, then they are scat-
tered among lesser objects of devotion like nation,
class, or race which come into open and subtle conflict.[54] Another consequence, says Niebuhr, is the
disintegration of self and society. [55] Personal and
social unities dissolve when the loyalties of self and
society are divided among a plurality of lesser interests and ideals. Self and society find themselves in
internal conflict when it happens that the pursuit of
one ideal necessarily conflicts with another.

As bad faith and a false attitude toward reality, worldliness issues in false patterns of moral behavior. Temptation to idolatry, to look upon life's
meaning as self-sufficient and self-contained, is
greater when humanity is surrounded by the work of its
own hands. In this situation, faith in self reigns
supreme. Despite plentiful evidence that the moral
order of the world is largely impervious to human
striving, the resolution of deep-seated personal and
social ills seems promised by yet another material or
ideal production of human mind and labor.

A key apprehension of this analysis, one but-
tressed by a pervasive loss of faith in social ideals
and institutions plainly unable to remedy economic disaster, is that secular culture "has a religion which,
like most religion, is bad--an idolatrous faith which
brings with it a train of moral consequences." [56]
Worldly faith appears in many forms.[57] What may be
called humanism, liberalism, or modernism is the most
pervasive form of modern idolatry. However, since each
of these terms also has more favorable meanings,
Niebuhr settles on "anthropocentrism" as the best,
comprehensive designation. [58]

Anthropocentric faith places humanity at the
center of the cosmos. Human desire becomes its source
of values and the cornerstone of its way of life.
Nationalism and capitalism are variant forms, since
one teaches people that their own country is "the ultimate worthful reality," while the other insists that
their economic production is the prime power and source
of life's meaning.[59] True religion recognizes the reference in all life to an absolute which transcends and
judges all experience of finite objects. By contrast,

28

anthropocentric movements elevate a finite entity (humanity, nation, wealth, industry) as the absolute referent for meaning and value.

For the purpose of Niebuhr's analysis, each supreme value or source of meaning constitutes a god which forms the basis for a fundamental orientation or way of life.[60] The ethical problem of the church is the result of its collaboration with anthropocentrism, a collaboration which threatens the integrity of its dominant loyalty and pattern of life. Christians are tempted to substitute social religion for faith in God.[61] "The captive church is the church which has become entangled with this system or these systems of worldliness. It is a church which seeks to prove its usefulness to civilization, in terms of civilization's own demands."[62]

The emancipation of the church begins with an affirmation of "the self-evident truth" that it and all life are dependent on God, and that loyalty to him is the condition for life.[63] This basic loyalty is the precondition for the integrity of the church, and it cannot be manufactured by an act of human will or striving. God's sovereignty and loyalty to him is faith's first certainty, without which neither Christian life nor theological criticism is possible.[64] For, "loyalties can be recognized as false only when a true loyalty has been discovered," and loyalty to God "is possible only by a reconciliation to God, which cannot be initiated by the disloyal creature."[65]

There are several important differences between The Social Sources of Denominationalism and Niebuhr's contributions to The Church Against the World. The earlier volume looks for an ideal for social ethics that can be detached from the mundane dynamics of history and also from explicit devotion to God. The later essays examine a faith-dimension of human life that constitutes a practical force in history and points beyond itself toward God. In Social Sources, the question is how the church can pursue the ideal of social unity. In The Church Against the World, it is how life's self-transcending tendency can be focused on the true God. The task of the church is no longer to fashion a more winsome portrait of the end of moral striving, but to ask how it can be true to its sovereign God. The ultimate question is whether human faith will be directed toward some finite object, including the ideal human fellowship, or whether it will point beyond these lesser objects to the transcendent Lord.

By 1935, Niebuhr's estimate of the relation between faith and ethics reaches a plainly Augustinian stage. Beneath the ideals, values, and actions of moral life, the basic issue is the orientation or direction of personal loyalty. Yet, reorientation can be accomplished only by a reconciliation initiated by God. The foundation of Christian morality, then, is not anthropocentric but theocentric. What is required is a loyalty founded on God's reconciling action that is consonant with the moral order of God's world. Repentance is necessary not because it serves the interests of civilization, but because "we are attacking the very son of God or God himself in our endeavor to escape suffering and to maintain our civilization at any cost."[66]

The task of the theologian is not to recommend allegiance to a new portrait of the ideal society. Exhortations of this kind fail to get at the root of the problem and also fall victim to the idolatrous suggestion that Christian faith is a utilitarian device to bring about civilization's cherished ends. Instead, the prior task is to point toward God since the first purpose of life is to serve him, and he alone can work the necessary change of heart. Reference to the living Lord is the _sine qua non_ of genuine Christian life.

A second task of the moral theologian is to extend the relevance of faith in God by showing how reconciliation shapes an identifiable design or pattern of moral life. A critical description of the Christian life compares its pattern with other skeins of life and loyalty. Comparison serves a dual purpose. On the one hand, it aids description by helping to identify distinctive features of the Christian life. On the other, it helps to clarify the relation between Christian faith and our social loyalties by showing how the Christian design supports and also challenges salient features of different worldly patterns.

Another way to describe this change in Niebuhr's theology is to say that belieful realism recasts the project of faith seeking understanding. In _Social Sources_, the dialectic of integrity and intelligibility is cast in idealist terms. The problem of integrity is the difficulty of constructing a portrait of the end of human striving that is true to biblical portraits of the kingdom. Intelligibility becomes the task of stating this ideal goal so that it synthesizes the highest social and ethical aspirations of western culture. If these requirements are met, the cultural and moral relevance of the biblically informed

30

ideal is clear. Talk about the kingdom is public talk about culture's highest ethical ideal.

But once the relevant sphere of moral inquiry is enlarged to include the dominant devotion of human personality, a different conception of faith seeking understanding begins to emerge. The first question is not "What is the ideal?" but "What is your dominant loyalty?" Integrity is from faith to faith. It is a judgment about the continuity between the faith of contemporary believers in God and the faith of the original witnesses that came to be expressed in biblical norms of human sinfulness and divine sovereignty.[67] The first answer of theological ethics is not the brotherhood of man or human solidarity, laudable as these ideals may be, but faith in the sovereignty of God and his reconciling action.

This new estimate of the foundation for Christian morality also requires a different understanding of intelligibility. Like integrity, intelligibility is also a complex determination about the faith dimension of Christian life and experience. The problem is no longer how a theological affirmation of a moral ideal can gain general assent. Instead, an intelligible account of Christian life requires that its dominant devotion and practical pattern be clearly described and critically compared with the fiduciary foundations and patterns of other forms of life. Comparison is based on a common structure of human devotion, and it enables an intelligent account of the difference Christian believing makes in personal and social life.

The possibility of showing how Christian faith influences moral life does not depend on a correspondence between the prime Christian motive for being moral and the incentives behind other systems of morality. Rather, since fundamental loyalties lie beneath and inform all patterns of moral life and their moral ideals, it is enough to describe loyalty to God as Christians understand it and to show how this loyalty affects and informs Christian morality. Surely, a critical comparison of the Christian design in moral life with other patterns will uncover significant similarities, among them similar moral ideals. But different moralities have distinct fiduciary foundations, and their values and ideals cannot be understood adequately without reference to their underlying faiths in some object(s).

For this reason, intelligibility requires clarity but not agreement. The nationalist can understand how the humanist reaches certain moral determinations without sharing the humanist's faith in the race, if only the humanist be clear about his basic loyalty and how it informs his morality. So also, the non-Christian can understand how the Christian reaches certain moral conclusions without sharing the Christian's faith, if only the Christian be clear about his dominant loyalty and the way it informs his life.

Notes

[1] CC, p. 43. See also James M. Gustafson, "Christian Ethics and Social Policy," Faith and Ethics: The Theology of H. Richard Niebuhr, ed. Paul Ramsey (New York: Harper and Row, Harper Torchbooks, 1957), p. 119. Niebuhr's effort to understand these relations was inaugurated earlier in articles like "Christianity and the Social Problem," Magazin für Evangelische Theologie und Kirche 50 (January 1922): 278-291: "Back to Benedict?" The Christian Century 42 (July 1925): 860-861; "What Holds the Churches Together?" The Christian Century 43 (March 1926): 346-348; "Christianity and the Industrial Classes," Theological Magazine of the Evangelical Synod of North America 57 (January 1929): 12-18; "Churches That Might Unite," The Christian Century 46 (February 1929): 259-261.

[2] Ernst Troeltsch, The Social Teaching of the Christian Churches, 2 vols., trans. Olive Wyon (New York: Harper and Brothers, Harper Torchbooks, 1960), 2:994-997. Troeltsch believes that his analysis sheds light on the dependence of Christian thought and dogma on basic social conditions. The two interact to form ideas of social fellowship and the church. See also SSD, p. 4.

[3] SSD, p. 6.

[4] Ibid., p. 13.

[5] Ibid., p. 25.

[6] Compare Niebuhr's statements about the effect of the church's compromise with the world and how the church becomes self-interested with Walter Rauschenbusch, A Theology for the Social Gospel, pp. 122, 144, 185-187.

[7] SSD, p. 6.

[8] Ibid., pp. 6-7.

[9] "Christianity and the Industrial Classes," p. 17.

[10] SSD, p. 273.

[11] Ibid., pp. 259-263.

[12] Ibid., pp. 106-108.

[13]Ibid., p. 279.

[14]Ibid., pp. 3, 264.

[15]Ibid., pp. 7-9, 22, 279. The same difficulty
is present in "Christianity and the Industrial Classes,"
where Niebuhr appeals to the realization of personal
dignity and worth that Christianity offers and describes salvation as deliverance from the selfishness
and unbrotherliness of men, pp. 15-16.

[16]SSD, p. 226.

[17]James W. Fowler, To See the Kingdom: The Theological Vision of H. Richard Niebuhr (Nashville:
Abingdon Press, 1974), p. 45.

[18]KGA, p. x. See also Walter Rauschenbusch, A
Theology for the Social Gospel, pp. 142-143; Francis G.
Peabody, Jesus Christ and the Social Question: An Examination of the Teaching of Jesus and its Relation to
Some of the Problems of Modern Social Life (New York:
Macmillan Company, 1903), pp. 120-121. Peabody says
that Jesus looks upon the world of social movement as
contributing to the social intention of the kingdom
of God.

[19]SSD, pp. 283-284. Rauschenbusch also emphasizes
human solidarity as an element of the kingdom. See
A Theology for the Social Gospel, p. 168. Shailer
Matthews regards "the sense of the solidarity of human
society" as a call for "the regeneration of the social
order" in his attempt to show that Jesus' message is
"consistent with the dominant presuppositions of today's thought and action." See The Gospel and the
Modern Man (New York: Macmillan Company, 1912), pp.
88-90.

[20]"Reformation: Continuing Imperative," p. 249.
Interestingly, Niebuhr does not include 1929, the year
he published The Social Sources of Denominationalism.

[21]Reinhold Niebuhr, "Must We Do Nothing?" The
Christian Century 49 (March 1932): 415. Also, compare
Reinhold Niebuhr's statements about a disinterested
Christian ethic that retains its independence from
culture with Richard's statements about the distinc-
tiveness of the Christian ethic in this time period.
It is interesting to note that both Niebuhrs found
Paul Tillich helpful in the thirties. See Reinhold
Niebuhr, An Interpretation of Christian Ethics (New

York: Seabury Press, A Crossroad Book, 1979), Preface, pp. 1-21.

[22]H. Richard Niebuhr, Moral Relativism and the Christian Ethic (New York: International Missionary Council, 1929), p. 4.

[23]Ibid., p. 8.

[24]H. Richard Niebuhr, "The Irreligion of Communist and Capitalist," The Christian Century 47 (October 1930): 1307.

[25]H. Richard Niebuhr, "Faith, Works, and Social Salvation," Religion in Life 1 (Summer 1932): 430.

[26]H. Richard Niebuhr, "Man the Sinner," The Journal of Religion 15 (July 1935): 272-273.

[27]H. Richard Niebuhr, "Religion and Ethics," The World Tomorrow 13 (November 1930): 443-446.

[28]Ibid., p. 445.

[29]Ibid.

[30]Ibid., p. 446. See also H. Richard Niebuhr, "Religious Realism in the Twentieth Century," Religious Realism, ed. Douglas Clyde Macintosh (New York: Macmillan Company, 1931), p. 240.

[31]"Religion and Ethics," p. 444.

[32]See Karl Barth, "The Problem of Ethics Today," The Word of God and the Word of Man, trans. Douglas Horton (New York: Harper and Row, Harper Torchbooks, 1957), pp. 177, 179.

[33]The movement is reflected in Douglas Clyde Macintosh, ed., Religious Realism; Reinhold Niebuhr, Moral Man and Immoral Society (New York: Charles Scribner's Sons, 1932); Reinhold Niebuhr, An Interpretation of Christian Ethics; Walter Marshall Horton, Realistic Theology (New York: Harper and Brothers, 1934).

[34]Douglas Clyde Macintosh, "Introduction," Religious Realism, ed. Douglas Clyde Macintosh, p. v.

[35]"Religious Realism in the Twentieth Century," pp. 414-415.

[36]Ibid., p. 416.

[37]Ibid., p. 418.

[38]Ibid., p. 420.

[39]Ibid.

[40]Paul Tillich, The Religious Situation, trans.
H. Richard Niebuhr (New York: Meridian Books, Living
Age Books, 1956), pp. 64-70.

[41]H. Richard Niebuhr, "Translator's Preface" to
Paul Tillich, The Religious Situation, p. 13.

[42]Ibid., p. 12. See also H. Richard Niebuhr,
"Life Is Worth Living," The Intercollegian and Far
Horizon 57 (October 1939): 4.

[43]"Translator's Preface" to Paul Tillich, The
Religious Situation, p. 12. See also Paul Tillich,
Systematic Theology, 3 vols. (Chicago: University of
Chicago Press, 1969) 1:238-247.

[44]H. Richard Niebuhr, "What Then Must We Do?"
The Christian Century Pulpit 5 (July 1934): 146. For
Reinhold Niebuhr also, questions about our confidence
in life, its form and meaning are raised by the failures and ills of contemporary society. See An Interpretation of Christian Ethics, p. 1.

[45]"Man the Sinner," p. 272.

[46]"What Then Must We Do?" p. 147.

[47]"Man the Sinner," p. 273. It may be instruc-
tive to compare this statement with Jonathan Edwards'
contention that the cause which determines the will
"is that motive, which as it stands in the view of the
mind, is strongest." All citations of Edwards' writings are from Jonathan Edwards, The Works of Jonathan
Edwards, 2 vols. (Carlisle, Pennsylvania: Banner of
Truth, 1834), hereafter cited as Works. The quotation
above is from "A Careful and Strict Enquiry into the
Prevailing Notions of the Freedom of the Will," Works,
1:5. For a brief description of Edwards' influence on
Niebuhr, see Leo Sandon, Jr., "Jonathan Edwards and H.
Richard Niebuhr," Religious Studies 12 (March 1976):
101-115.

[48]CAW, p. 4.

[49] Ibid., p. 12.

[50] Ibid., p. 4.

[51] Ibid., p. 125.

[52] Ibid.

[53] Ibid.

[54] H. Richard Niebuhr, "Nationalism, Socialism and Christianity," The World Tomorrow 16 (August 1933): 469.

[55] "Man the Sinner," p. 279.

[56] CAW, p. 127; "What Then Must We Do?" p. 146.

[57] CAW, p. 126.

[58] Ibid., p. 136.

[59] Ibid., p. 130. Niebuhr regards the Marxist interpretation of history as the reductive product and statement of the "economic faith." As such, communism is a variant form of "capitalistic religion." A similar assessment of communism appears in "The Irreligion of Communist and Capitalist," pp. 1306-1307.

[60] CAW, pp. 128-136.

[61] Ibid., pp. 137-138.

[62] Ibid., p. 138.

[63] Ibid., p. 149.

[64] Ibid.

[65] "Man the Sinner," p. 279.

[66] H. Richard Niebuhr, "Utilitarian Christianity," Christianity and Crisis 6 (July 1946): 5.

[67] "Reformation: Continuing Imperative," p. 248.

CHAPTER III

FAITH, HISTORY, AND THEOLOGY

As is well known, Niebuhr himself takes pains
to distinguish his method in The Kingdom of God in
America from his procedure in The Social Sources of
Denominationalism.[1] The later volume is a reappraisal
of the history of American Christianity in light of the
beliefully realistic connection between loyalty to a
valued object and the morphology of practical life. It
differs from Social Sources because it attends especially to the faith dimension of Christian life.

The earlier, social history of American Christianity attends to the instrumental value of religion
for society. It shows how religion functions to forti-
fy the morale of individuals and groups, to defend self
and society from disillusionment and doubt.[2] This perspective so clearly offers a "true interpretation of so
much that happens in religion" that one hesitates to
exempt any part of religion from its scope.[3] But the
instrumental value of faith for society depends on
faith's conviction that it has more than instrumental
value. "Faith could not defend men if it believed that
defense was its meaning."[4]

The fact that Niebuhr takes up a different
standpoint in The Kingdom of God in America does not
mean that he repudiates the social perspective of the
earlier volume, though he rejects its theological conclusion. We cannot keep from analyzing complex historical movements from diverse perspectives precisely because their historical expressions are so clearly influenced by diverse factors. Different interpretations
can be compared in order to take this complexity into
account and to obtain a fuller picture.[5] But a social
view fails to see the impact of believing in God as
religious people see it. It sees only what are incidental results of faith in God from a Christian viewpoint. Similarly, a theological interpretation of the
modern labor movement is apt to focus on what are only
incidental results of a commitment to labor reform from
an economic perspective. The point is simply that each
historical movement, whether political, economic, or
religious, has a dominant loyalty or conviction that
engages external forces and has some impact upon them.
Thus, "no movement can be understood until its presuppositions, the fundamental faith on which it rests,
have been at least provisionally adopted."[6]

From the perspective of its dominant loyalty, Christianity is a dynamic force engaged in the push and shove of history. In its converse with other loyalties and commitments which influence human life and behavior, it comes to diverse historical expressions; now adjusting to new surroundings, now adjusting new surroundings to suit itself. If Social Sources employs history to show that Christians have fallen away from a static, original ideal of organic solidarity, the new approach regards Christian faith as a Protean thing.[7] What we are to notice is not a constancy of moral ideals, but a vital stream of historical faith which gives rise to moral expressions. The question is whether we can discern a meaningful pattern in the ebb and flow of Christian faith through its American environment.

In The Kingdom of God in America, then, belieful realism has a dual significance. It refers to the interpreter's conviction that the faith dimension of human life points beyond itself to transcendent reality, but it also describes the basic presupposition of the Christian movement. Both the interpreter and the object of interpretation perceive themselves to be in dialogue with the sovereign God. In fact, the investigator is trying to discover the turns which that conversation has taken in the past. He is like "a sailor who seeks to find his bearings by consulting the charts his fathers used when they set out on the voyage he is continuing."[8]

The Story of American Faith

For Niebuhr, Protestantism is America's primary religion, and its features can be discerned only against the background of medieval Catholicism.[9] The medieval church conceives God as the changeless perfection from which all things proceed and to which they return. Mundane reality is, therefore, engaged in the process of returning to eternity; its dominant impulse is to pursue the eternal vision of the perfect deity.[10]

Metaphysically, this motif comes to expression in conceptions of the great chain of being, teleologically ordered toward eternity. Each being constitutes a link which is closer or further from the perfect source and end of all things. The order of society follows a corresponding hierarchical plan. The divine rule is refracted through a chain of social authority. Persons and organizations are responsible to the next link in the feudal structure. Personal life is also ordered toward the contemplative vision of God as its last end

or goal. Pursuit of changeless perfection through preparatory activity within the hierarchical scheme of nature and society defines the skein of personal existence.[11] For the medieval Christian, visio dei is not
just a comforting opinion; it is an authentic apprehension of known reality which penetrates the possibilities and limitations of practical life.[12]

A different religious paradigm emerges during
the Reformation. Protestantism exchanges visio dei for
regnum dei and so precipitates a redescription of God,
humanity, and the world.[13] On this model, God is king,
and the world is his kingdom. Divine reality administers the world directly, without recourse to a hierarchy of being. Thus, Luther and Calvin construe God
more as active power than as changeless perfection, and
they emphasize his sovereign will more than his eternal
being.

Protestant conceptions of social authority reflect this different image of the ultimate environment.
Plans for a stable social hierarchy are thought to be
fundamentally flawed. Instead, all human organizations
are directly responsible to God, and society is understood as a multiplicity of equals.[14] Personal existence becomes a matter of obedient response to prior
divine action more than a preparatory pursuit of contemplative perfection. Obedience to God's will within
the moral economy of direct responsibility to him defines the dominant skein for practical life.

For the Protestant emerging from feudal patri-
mony, regnum dei expresses a new vision of life's possibilities and limitations which challenges the old
order. It expresses the apprehension that divine will
is directly available to individuals and groups. It
communicates the sense that the kingdom is at hand and
that judgment is imminent. Thus, the new movement
challenges medieval habits and institutions "in the
name of the very universal and eternal truth which
they claimed to represent."[15]

But the new image also creates considerable
difficulties. By criticizing absolute ecclesiastical
power, it clears the way for secular government, economic institutions, and emancipated individuals to
claim ultimate authority.[16] Reliance on God's self-
revelation threatens moral life with a lack of precision, since it offers no specific criteria for choosing
"between relative goods and relative evils."[17] The
insistence that Christ alone is head of the church

opens the door to "self-appointed spokesmen for God."[18] The problem of the early church reemerges. How can Christians be loyal citizens of God's kingdom in the world?[19]

Niebuhr distinguishes three Protestant answers to this question. Each represents a type of constructive Protestantism which supports a different form of life. Lutherans emphasize the theory of the two kingdoms. In spiritual matters, the loyal Christian gives sovereignty to God and relies on his word. In the temporal realm, however, Luther apparently assumes that God's rule is adequately reflected by the present social order.[20] Thus, Lutherans tend to concentrate on the freedom of the word in spiritual matters, but to yield temporal authority to political and economic powers.

By contrast, Calvinists reject the theory of two kingdoms and tend to restrain all human agencies and powers. Church and state are relatively independent of each other, but subject to the same godly constitution. No part of human life, whether political, spiritual, ecclesiastical, or economic is beyond God's universal reign.[21] Finally, sectarians tend to resolve the problem of construction by distinguishing God's coming kingdom from the present kingdoms of this world. Devotion to the coming kingdom is then thought to require moral stringency within the believing community as well as its self-sufficiency and independence from political and economic life.

While Protestants in Europe forge these constructive options in conflict and compromise with the old order, the history of the Protestant movement in America is distinguished by the absence of an established order to protest.[22] For Niebuhr, the contours of American experience can be arranged into three main periods characterized respectively by social construction, practical individualism, and national optimism as their leading themes. In each period, the interaction between Protestant faith in the God who acts and historical circumstances yields a different expression of regnum dei, and the resultant expression of the Protestant paradigm has an impact on the way Christians construe the leading features of American experience.

According to Niebuhr, a perception of divine sovereignty dominates the Protestant movement during the first period of American history. For Puritans, Quakers, and separatists, God administers his kingdom

42

as its absolute monarch. He is intimately connected
with ordinary as well as extraordinary events. When
this perception of divine activity interacts with the
pressing issue of social construction, the result is a
symbolic specification of regnum dei as the divine
commonwealth which people inhabit and on which they
depend. 23

Though the different parties disagree on the
particulars of an appropriate social order, their unity
comes to expression in three corollaries of divine sovereignty: Christian constitutionalism, the independence
of the church, and the limitation of power. Constitutionalism means that revelation is the basis for organizing life within the divine commonwealth. Puritans
stress the objective standard of God's will in scripture, while Quakers and separatists emphasize the subjective experience of the Holy Spirit. But Puritans
acknowledge the importance of the Spirit in biblical
interpretation, and Quakers and separatists are "per-
meated with scriptural ideas."24 Thus, the understanding of revelation adopted by the movement as a whole
reflects the classical dialectic of the Spirit and the
Letter.

The independence of the church means that the
believing community depends on God alone.25 No single
institutional design emerges from this principle, but,
again, the movement as a whole reflects a classical
dialectic of Christian faith: the dual direction of
Christian vocation. Wary of the dangers of separation
from the world, Puritans attempt a synthesis of this
dual impulse. Quakers and separatists stress withdrawal from the world but remain conscious of mission.
Colonial Christianity in America moves along a curious
path, never quite resolving the institutional question
into the European alternatives of state church and
otherworldly sect.26

Finally, the limitation of power expresses the
necessity of restraining the tendency of human power to
exalt itself rather than the sovereign Lord.27 All parties remain suspicious of power whether in the hands of
clergy, royalty, aristocracy, or the people. All agree
that the people are the mundane source of political
power. But Puritans limit the power of free men by
divine ordinances, while Quakers and separatists subject it to inner restraints. Because conscience derives its authority from its ability to apprehend laws
of the divine commonwealth, not conscience but the
reality it discerns is absolute.28

The importance of Niebuhr's analysis is that it suggests a dynamic pattern by which Protestant faith develops on American soil. Puritans, Quakers, and separatists extend the relevance of their belief in God by interpreting God's kingdom through their experience and their experience through the symbol of God's kingdom. As this symbol, which is drawn from the Bible and is prominent in the Protestant heritage, interacts with colonial experience, a vision of the divine commonwealth and its intermediate principles begins to emerge. By means of this vision, American Protestants spell out a pattern of life and loyalty which relates the transcendent God to mundane realities and orients the varied dimensions of life in accordance with their perception of the sovereign Lord. Their vision becomes an active force in colonial history. It affirms and also challenges early American tendencies toward institutional traditionalism and the individualistic authority of conscience.[29] It both interprets and corrects the sensibilities of colonists engaged in the business of building their new society, and thus becomes an intelligible symbolization of life's possibilities and limitations.

During the Great Awakening and the revivals, a perception of divine grace comes to the fore. The Christian movement faces a new society of emancipated individuals on a frontier of cheap land and relaxed social conventions. The image of a kingdom of Christ intimately connected with personal experience emerges as faith's perception of grace interacts with this new environment.

Thus, the evangelists conceive Christ's kingdom as a rule of self-restraint in repentant persons.[30] Though this image differs from the earlier portrait of God's commonwealth ruled by ecclesiastical and political covenants, it too presupposes an apprehension of divine sovereignty. The common apprehension of Edwards, Wesley, Whitefield, and Finney is that human will is always loyal to something and in its fallen state, loyal to something other than the universal good.[31] The problem is "not the discovery of an adequate ideal nor the generation of will whereby ideals might be realized, but rather the redirection of the will to live."[32]

The nature of this redirection is reconciliation to God as the true good, a turning from self toward the universal being. As the continuing action of God in history, Christ's incarnation makes entrance

44

into his kingdom possible. Redirection is enabled by
what Edwards calls "converting influences" and what
Archibald Alexander calls "spiritual knowledge" or
"saving faith."[33] Christ's kingdom is reconciliation
to God enabled by God's action in Christ and worked by
God's converting influence on the Christian.

According to Niebuhr, this emphasis improves
earlier understandings of revelation. The insistence
that the reign of Christ is a rule of knowledge mediated to people through the experience of grace combines
objective and subjective criteria.[34] Revivalists maintain the divine initiative in revelation and affirm the
Bible as the objective standard by which all experience
is to be judged. But they also insist that what is objective and historical needs to be made subjective and
contemporary through experience. This enables leaders
of the religious enlightenment to use the Bible with
greater freedom than did the Puritans and with greater
fidelity than did earlier exponents of "inner light."[35]
They strike a delicate balance between scripture and
experience which remains influential.[36]

The evangelical view of reconciliation also
joins affective conviction with an intellectual discernment of God's relation to mundane reality. The
knowledge that God is related to all things supports
Woolman's universal love to fellow creatures, Edwards'
true virtue, Wesley's reverence for life, and Hopkins'
principle of disinterested benevolence.[37] Just as the
Puritan believed good works to be the best evidence of
genuine holiness, so Edwards and the revivalists emphasize Christian practice and works of charity.[38]

This brings a second major contribution of the
evangelical movement into view. The Great Awakening
and the revivals combine the dual impulses of Christian
vocation. Whereas different parties tend toward separation and involvement during the colonial period, now
a centrist group emerges which tries to comprehend
withdrawal and involvement in a single dynamic movement. For the revivalists, the first consequence of
spiritual experience is a new tendency toward withdrawal. Thus, they distinguish their main purpose from
politics and also revitalize the principle of converted
membership.[39] But "the essence of the new awakening to
the reign of Christ" is "in faith working by love."[40]
Reconciliation also supports a renewed tendency toward
mission. Sunday schools flourish, as do colleges and
secondary schools established by religious groups.
Voluntary societies founded by people with religious

inspirations and committed to a variety of reforms become plentiful.[41]

Again, Niebuhr's analysis shows American Christians involved in a loose process of development and interpretation. The symbol of Christ's kingdom is true to biblical apprehensions of human sin, divine sovereignty, and grace. It expresses the theme of grace in a way that is true to the Reformation heritage. At the same time, however, it is no mere repetition of past symbolic formulas but emerges in interaction with the American experience of independence. Out of this interactive milieu, principles like reconciliation and vocation begin to emerge. In light of these principles, Christians chart a relation between transcendent and mundane reality that orients life according to their perception of God's grace. Their vision supports and also challenges American tendencies toward practical individualism. It affirms the importance of personal experience, but insists that this experience derives authority from its objective discernment of God's involvement in the world. It affirms the importance of practice, but also elicits a commitment to serve others for Christ's sake. By engaging distinct features of American experience, it becomes an intelligible guide to possibilities and limitations in a new society under God.

Hope for God's coming kingdom sounds a minor theme during the colonial period. Nevertheless, hoped-for immortality distinguishes the present order from the future order of glory and contributes to a sense of the relativity of social institutions. More prophetic conceptions of society emerge among Puritans, however, when the coming kingdom is connected with God's present rule and political upheavals elicit a sense of crisis in social life.

For the Quaker, hope is closely connected with the experience of inner light. He tends to interpret social decay and disaster as a divine judgment on the world's corruption, as when Fox sees blood in the market place and streets of Lichfield while he listens for the final trumpet.[42] But the Quaker's hope can also be infiltrated by the claim that the kingdom has already come to those who have experienced the Spirit of Christ. Indeed, the Quaker sometimes plays the perfectionist unwilling to adjust his absolute ethic to the restraint of evil in an unredeemed world. As tensions mount, he is forced either to relinquish his faith or his participation in public life.[43]

Near the end of the colonial period, deism and social complacency lessen expectations of the kingdom. But hopes for redemption revitalize when they are connected with convictions of divine power and grace during the Great Awakening and the revivals. Now the kingdom appears not only as the eternal bliss people might lose, but also as the threat they cannot escape.[44] Christ enables people to anticipate the coming kingdom both in threat and promise.[45]

Like Woolman, Americans of the eighteenth and nineteenth centuries anticipate the kingdom in their hearts by "dying and rising with Christ."[46] Like Edwards, they believe that surprising works of God's spirit signal the new creation.[47] But unlike earlier Quakers, they preserve the tension toward the future. Edwards is a millenarian who thinks present manifestations of Christ's kingdom will fall short of perfection. Hopkins believes that Christ's reign is still future, while Wesley thinks the present revival is the beginning of a far greater work and refuses to calculate the end time.[48]

During the nineteenth century, the perception of God's redeeming action confronts naturalistic visions of human sovereignty, nationalistic portraits of manifest destiny, and capitalistic anticipations of industrial triumph.[49] God's coming kingdom emerges as faith's dominant expression in the midst of this ethos of optimism. In New England, the mantle of prophetic hope falls to a group of religious humanists who sometimes detach the kingdom from sovereignty and grace. Nevertheless, William Ellery Channing insists that "Christ comes in the conversion, the regeneration, the emancipation of the world."[50] Motivated at least in part by the sense that Christ's spirit requires a concern for love and justice in social life, he supports philanthropy and the abolition of slavery and war.[51]

Outside New England, the coming kingdom is closely bound to evangelical and humanitarian enterprises which grew out of the revivals. Alexander Campbell calls for the end of church divisions, the extension of public education, the elimination of legal injustice, and the emancipation of slaves. Theodore Weld regards revivals, moral reform, temperance, women's rights, and antislavery movements as parts of the same whole.[52]

But Christian hope shows its greatest difference with the reigning cultural optimism by its insis-

tence that the coming kingdom is judgment as well as
promise. For the cultural optimist, the abolition of
slavery is a step toward realization of the kingdom on
earth. To revivalists, it is a needed step of repentance, a preparation for the wrath to some. Finney insists on restitution. Weld proclaims that "prejudice
has spurned God's image," iniquity has "cursed the poor
and blasphemed God," and "the land is full of blood."[53]

Samuel Harris systematizes evangelical hope in
The Kingdom of Christ on Earth. Rejecting literal mil-
lenarianism as well as its humanistic forms, he insists
that the coming kingdom is life changed at its center
and in all its social relations. It is the product of
"a redeeming power [that] comes down upon humanity from
God, quickening men to spiritual life and transforming
society into the kingdom of God."[54]

For nineteenth century Protestants, as for the
colonists and revivalists before them, the dominant
vision that emerges from the interaction of faith and
experience includes intermediate principles. Dependence on God means that the coming kingdom is advanced
by divine power more than human striving.[55] Conversion, a principle borrowed from the evangelists, means
that this divine power regenerates the central principle in humanity.[56] Divine energy makes human work
effective through reconciliation. Finally, what we
might call the principle of pressing into the kingdom
means that regenerated agents work to extend liberty
to all people.

With the aid of this vision, the dynamic perception of God's kingdom is brought to bear on every
aspect of life. Nineteenth century Protestantism affirms but also judges the expectant optimism of nineteenth century America. If activist Christianity is
optimistic about the future, says Niebuhr, its optimism
springs from confidence in the promises of God rather
than a celebration of human sovereignty. Its representatives insist that the coming kingdom is a moral order
and not simply one of human fulfillment, national triumph, or industrial success. This fact, coupled with
American failures to observe it, leads some within the
Christian movement to emphasize repentance and the perception that the coming kingdom is crisis.

Discerning a Pattern

As the stream of faith moves through American
history, there is a loose interplay between images of

God furnished by the tradition and the believer's present experience. The _regnum dei_ paradigm, which emerges in the Reformation, expresses a predominantly biblical apprehension of God as an active power who creates, sustains, judges, and redeems.[57] In creative periods, American Christians interpret this symbol in light of their experience and interpret their experience in light of this symbol. As image and experience are fitted together, a dynamic vision of life in relation to God begins to emerge.

But creative periods are often followed by periods of stagnation. Indeed, for Niebuhr, the alternation between dynamism and petrification, a pattern he borrows from Henri Bergson, seems present throughout the history of faith in God.[58] The convictions of prophets are conserved by legal Judaism in a way that erodes the vitality of prophetic faith. Greek and Roman churches institutionalize the living faith of the apostolic period. Later scholasticism freezes the renaissance of the twelfth and thirteenth centuries. State churches, systems of pure doctrine, and conventional conduct crystallize continental Protestantism. In needed attempts to preserve their religious heritage, heirs of Puritan settlers introduce the Half-Way Covenant and Quakers discover birthright membership.[59]

For later Puritans, the sovereignty of God is no longer his living rule experienced in each moment, but an indirect administration by laws. The perception of a living reality behind the principles of the dependence of the church and the limitation of human power falters. Instead, the divine commonwealth becomes a virtually absolute institution to be conserved.

The experience of grace in the Great Awakening and the revivals revivifies a sense of urgent personal relations with God and also the perception of divine sovereignty. But it too is followed by a new conventional faith. Lyman Beecher views God as a distant monarch who administers his kingdom through unchanging laws established in nature and published in scripture. Biblicism fractures the dialectic of scripture and experience. The Bible becomes a book of static laws "rather than an aid to the understanding of God's living will."[60]

The corruption of divine sovereignty transmutes faith's sense of dependence and its tendency toward obedient activity into the logical paradox of divine determinism and human freedom. Debates ensue, with one side insisting that God does not wholly determine and the other embracing fatalism. "When the sovereignty of God has been reduced to a code of laws established in the past all the ideas associated with it at a time when it was experienced as a living reality become unintelligible."[61]

Similarly, the petrification of grace and of Christ's kingdom follow the Great Awakening and the revivals. Missions are divided along denominational lines. Reforming societies confuse themselves with their cause and promote the dominant conventions of their own group. The church comes to regard itself as the sole agent of God's grace and moral government, the only "practical system for accomplishing the salvation of the world."[62] Like a symbol that has lost its saltness, the church convinced of its exclusive contract points to itself.

The post-revival period also presides over the nationalization of Christ's kingdom. America becomes "a chosen nation especially favored."[63] The crisis of regeneration is past. "It occurred in the democratic revolution, or in the birth of modern science, or in the evangelical revival, or in the Protestant Reformation."[64] Faith becomes an American possession whose fruits are mediated to the world through the ministrations of an Anglo-Saxon empire. Revivalisms replace revivals. As the sole agents of grace, the American churches usurp divine initiative by translating regeneration into a prescribed method of conversion.[65]

When the grace of God has been reduced to a method, the principles associated with it at a time when it was unexpectedly experienced become unintelligible. Spiritual experience dissolves into American subjectivity. The dialectic of vocation is frozen, since the culture Christians once sought to convert itself becomes God's preferred instrument. To be reconciled to God now means to be reconciled to the prevalent mores and attitudes of Christian America and to foster its national aspirations to industrial success.

Finally, petrification also assails the religious perception of redemption. Fundamentalists translate individual salvation into a remote, otherworldly event. Judgment is trivialized as it comes to mean the deserts of those who fail to observe institutionalized laws. Heaven becomes "a reward for good deeds alone," and hope for the kingdom is transformed into a moral sanction for ecclesiastical, economic, and political

advancement.[66]   The anticipation of crisis becomes a
strategy for proselytizing new members.   In social
affairs, faith in God's coming kingdom translates into
a belief in progress.   Hope anticipates no crisis.
The divine power advancing the kingdom has already
descended, affording Americans the opportunity to extend their institutions to the world.   Even the youthful Bushnell identifies complete Protestantism with
pure Christianity, pure congregationalism with complete
Protestantism, and pure congregationalism as the author
of the American republic.[67]

The American ascendance to dominion over history completes the corruption of redemption and eliminates the sense of crisis.   The idea that America
might encounter the coming kingdom as judgment, or that
American churches might pass through new crucifixions,
becomes unthinkable.   No urgent repentance is needed.
No further catastrophe seems possible.   The coming
kingdom, whether conceived in ecclesiastical, political, or economic terms, is the "completion of tendencies now established."[68]   God's kingdom has been reduced to the goal of national striving.

For Niebuhr, conservative movements crystallize
the symbols, creeds, and formulas of a previous generation hoping to preserve their insights.   To some degree,
they succeed.   But they also jeopardize the vitality of
faith by fastening it to static symbolic forms.   Faith
in God becomes increasingly trivial.   "What could truly
be said of a living process becomes untrue or unintelligible when it is asserted of the petrified product."[69]
Moreover, by attending to the symbol more than its
meaning, conservative movements also threaten faith's
integrity.   The crystallized formulas of a creative
period omit what can never be captured, namely, the
living perception of God that originally gave rise
to the symbol.   Thus, conservative movements finally
change the content which they are trying to preserve;
they deny what they wish to affirm.[70]

What Niebuhr calls "dynamic liberalism" emerges
as an alternative to orthodox stasis.[71]   Channing,
Emerson, and Bellamy represent a faith in God that sees
all the world as sacred, enlivens sentiments, and leads
to action.   Emerson is more interested in being reno-
vated and "lifted to some higher platform" than in the
moralistic observance of meticulous custom.[72]   As a
whole, dynamic liberalism also shares dynamic evangel-
icalism's attitude toward the future.   This species
of liberal optimism, says Niebuhr, has its source in

51

biblical prophets and apostles.[73] It is a non-nationalized hope that leads people to press into the kingdom, devising utopian experiments and religious associations from Brook Farms to the Philadelphians.

But if liberalism revitalizes some aspects of faith's classical perceptions, it also tends to neglect others. There is a tendency to establish continuity between God and man by humanizing God and deifying humanity. No deep sin plagues. No transition from God the enemy to God the friend seems necessary. Undynamic liberalism reconciles the interests of individuals and societies too easily, and neglects the perversion of misguided loyalties to nation, class, and self. Since there is no deep corruption to be healed, liberal interpretations of Christ's kingdom are short on sacrifice. Restoration comes to mean the nurture of kindly affections and the extension of humanitarian ideals already dominant in the human breast. To be sure, liberalism's best representatives do not identify the growth of these sentiments and ideals with the destiny of the nation. Instead, the progress of "civilization" (often a euphemism for western culture) takes the place of the Christian revolution.[74]

When people qualify divine sovereignty, conceive grace as a remedy with no disease to heal, and picture redemption as continuous organic growth, the continuity of their faith with scripture and the Protestant tradition becomes dubious. This is one way to interpret Niebuhr's statement that for liberalism, "a God without wrath brought men without sin into a kingdom without judgment through the ministrations of a Christ without a cross."[75] But it is equally valid to note that when we excise these disjunctive elements from our religious vision, we can no longer make adequate sense of the undeniable discontinuities in our ordinary experience.

Of course, there are mediators who share the liberal protest against static orthodoxy and also try to retain the dialectical elements of Protestant faith. Horace Bushnell's reflections on the atonement presuppose the virulence of sin and confront what Niebuhr calls "the discontinuities of life" and the "revolutionary elements of Christianity."[76] Walter Rauschenbusch continues to emphasize conversion and the belief that the coming kingdom is crisis as well as fulfillment.[77] But "no mediating theology in history", says Niebuhr, "has ever been able to keep in balance the opposing elements it seeks to reconcile."[78] The

mediating tradition in America suffers a progressive
loss of religious heritage.

For Niebuhr, liberalizing movements try to revitalize religious perceptions by communicating them in
new symbolic forms. To some degree, they succeed. But
the unintended consequence is to jeopardize the integrity of faith by exchanging its past expressions too
easily and uncritically for new symbols which harmonize
with contemporary values but fail to transform them.
Liberalism finally evolves a precarious doctrine in
need of an apologetic to demonstrate its social
relevance and utility.[79]

Precisely when the integrity of liberal faith
and its continuity with the religious heritage become
dubious, its relevance and intelligibility are also
called into question. Removed from the language and
sometimes also the affections of the tradition, liberal
faith threatens to dissolve into a mere reflection of
present cultural attitudes. Thus, its apologists are
often hard pressed to give an intelligible account of
what difference it makes to believe in God. Moreover,
by promoting the dominant purposes and values of their
age or group, liberals tend to fashion religious visions plainly unable to account for the disjunctions
in experience which resist our social, national, and
economic loyalties. The oft experienced failures of
our anthropocentric faiths remain uninterpreted. Thus,
for example, when experience is interpreted exclusively
by a model of organic growth uninterrupted by revolutionary divine activity, not only sin, regeneration,
and judgment, but also national disaster become
unintelligible.

The alternation between dynamism and petrification that Niebuhr discerns in both orthodox and liberal
movements suggests an important dialectic. When the
vital connection between faith's genuine symbolic expressions and its lived experience falters, the Christian movement stagnates. An adequate religious vision
must, therefore, be true to faith's biblical expressions and also intelligible to faith's present experience. If an image of God and the world violates normative biblical expressions, e.g., an unrelieved model of
organic growth, there is little reason to think that it
will enable believers to identify a pattern in their
own experience that discloses the same transcendent
reality perceived by the biblical communities. The
historic continuity of Christian believing is then
called into question. Moreover, if one assumes that

the God perceived by the biblical communities remains
the sovereign Lord of our present, then a skewed perception of that God leads to a misunderstanding of our
present experience. Loss of integrity leads to a corresponding loss of intelligibility.

A symbolization that neglects faith's present
experience precipitates similar difficulties. First,
it furnishes confused and incomplete interpretations of
contemporary experience which obscure Christian life
and practice. An unintelligible vision cannot generate
a coherent or informative portrait of life and action
in relation to God. But if one assumes that the biblical communities believed their perception of God to be
an apprehension of a sovereign reality relevant to
every aspect of life, then an unintelligible vision is
also untrue to the biblical witness. It lacks integrity precisely because it frustrates relevance of believing in God and fails to provide an adequate vision
of present life. In short, integrity and intelligibility are mutual prerequisites for faith's legitimate and
dynamic development.

The implication of this discovery seems clear.
In order to facilitate faith's dynamic development, the
theologian must retrieve its classical expressions and
also give them new life in the present. He must grasp
both horns of the interpretative dilemma. For Niebuhr,
this means that divine sovereignty is the first venerable
truth in need of an intelligible exposition.

Faith and Value

In "Value Theory and Theology," Niebuhr attacks
liberalism's implicit rejection of divine sovereignty
and suggests how this classical affirmation of Christian faith can be coherently conceived in the modern
world. [80] Liberal theologies generally assume that
people have some knowledge of absolutely valid values
that is independent of their knowledge of God. Left-
wing Hegelians and radical Ritschlians define God as
the highest value supported by human wishes, desires,
or ideals. Kantians tend to view divine attributes as
those qualities of transcendent reality necessary to
support our independent knowledge of the highest good.
Empirical theologians, like Douglas Clyde Macintosh and
Henry Nelson Wieman, define God in light of universally
valid ends. [81] In each case, prior affirmations of
value determine the reality of God.

For Niebuhr, this approach is scientifically

inadequate precisely because it predetermines the results of theological inquiry. One major achievement
of modern science is to train attention on the object
under investigation. The hallmark of modern empirical
inquiry is its freedom from the hegemony of the pre-
arranged hierarchy of values into which its medieval
predecessor tried to "fit" observed facts. But a theological pseudo-science that investigates reality in
light of prior values, like mind, personality, and
spirituality, has already decided which observations
are significant and which are not. It predetermines
the significance of the facts and tends to substitute
contrived teleological explanations of nature for
scientific descriptions that conflict with its pre-
arranged system of values.[82] In short, the procedures
of liberal value-theology are at odds with scientific
method in the modern world.

Such a theology becomes dependent on prevailing
systems of ethics and captive to an interest in its own
value from other viewpoints. It, therefore, exchanges
its independence and integrity for social utility. But
no scientific inquiry worthy of the name can long with-
stand direction at the behest of its social usefulness.
A theology that borrows its first principles from other
disciplines forfeits the originality of its viewpoint
and so also any prospect for new knowledge. Ironic-
ally, by seeking to justify its own social value, it
becomes a bad science which yields few beneficial
results.[83]

Second, liberal value-theologies are religiously unsatisfactory since religion itself "demands that
God be loved for his own sake."[84] A reduction of God
to a means for maintaining social values threatens the
integrity of worship. When theological portraits of
God arbitrarily favor personal qualities over universality, power, and unity, it also becomes increasingly
difficult to relate God's rule to impersonal aspects of
nature and to account for the givenness and limitations
of human life. Thus, religious ethics departs from a
tradition that founds morality on the sole value of God
and his creatures precisely because they are his creatures. A "religionism" arises which directs attention
to the value maintaining and promoting character of
faith for society. The incidental by-products of faith
that are valuable for culture take priority over its
main affirmations, and religion points to itself rather
than the sovereign God.[85]

Theologies that determine God and his actions

with respect to prior values also tend to neglect the historical particularity of religious faith. They are heirs "of that rationalism which sought to go back of the historical, individual faiths to a general, rational religion available to all men."[86] Having discovered the essence of religion in absolute values apart from historical faith in God, they make devotion to these values more important than worship of the beings with which the historic faiths are concerned. As individual religions reduce to examples of humanity's common faith, the classical claim that historic revelation discloses the universal reality to which human values must conform becomes unintelligible.[87]

Finally, theologies that determine God with reference to prior values are philosophically inadequate. They confuse religious faith with affirmations of moral values. The dogmas of ethics, says Niebuhr, like the self-evident goodness of a good will, of pleasure, or personality or of personal life, are religious dogmas. "They are assertions of faith, confessions of trust in something that makes life worth living, commitments of the self to a god."[88] To found religion on one of these assertions is not to lend it an undogmatic, rational foundation, but to confound the integrity of one faith with another.

Liberal value theologies also deny the philosophical principle of relativity since they fail to take seriously the standpoints from which their values appear absolute. Extreme idealists who absolutize values that are allegedly independent of human mind and nature fail to account for the standpoint of the observer. Ritschlians absolutize values that are relative to human spirituality. American empiricists initially appear to be exceptions to the rule, since they regard value as a characteristic of all and not just human reality. But Macintosh absolutizes values that are valid for all persons, while Wieman equates God with the structure of the universe that sustains and promotes the human good.[89]

To make values relative to human personality the criteria for divine reality is to assume that God is the guarantor of personal ends, to have confidence in a harmony between the values of human personality and the values of God. When theology conceives a unified system of reality in which value proceeds harmoniously from the lower to the higher, from the individual to the universal, then classical ideas of broken relations between persons and nature and between persons

56

and God are lost. The conflict and tragedy of values
in our ordinary experience becomes unintelligible.[90]
For Niebuhr, however, the values relative to animal
life are only occasionally included in the system of
human values.[91] More often, animal life is sacrificed
to human ends. Only occasionally are values relative
to individuals in harmony with values relative to societies. Ordinarily, "the social values require the
sacrifice of the values of isolated personality and
vice versa."[92] The situation is similar with respect
to relations between persons and God. Only occasionally are values relative to isolated humanity harmonious
with the goodness and justice of divine reality. A
more realistic and satisfactory theological science
will not gloss over conflict and tragedy in the name
of progressive integration.[93]

At this point, the neo-Reformation theologies
offer an important corrective. They rightly insist
that revelation precipitates a crisis in human life.
But they fail to offer an intelligible account of how
revelation is received precisely because they refuse to
relate revelation to human values in any way. By setting revelation completely apart from human faiths in
other objects of value, they fail to describe intelligibly its impact on practical life. The assertion of
God's sovereignty and the denial that people possess
valid prior standards by which to judge God and his
self-disclosure are true to religious experience.

But assertion and denial are not enough in
theology. The theologian is required to show
where and how such denials and assertions have
been made possible, and how they compare with
the assertions and denials of other faiths.[94]

For Niebuhr, religion may be intelligibly interpreted as "an affair of valuation" without assuming
that religious valuation is based on a known standard
established prior to religious experience.[95] To do so
requires a theory of values which recognizes that value
is relative to "the human constitution and its actual
needs," but independent of "human desire and the consciousness of need."[96] Such a theory accommodates the
religious insight that God creates humanity with an
objective, structural need for himself, but it also
recognizes that our human consciousness of this need
has been skewed and corrupted.

In general, values emerge in relations among
beings.[97] Thus, for example, a father's care for his

child is perceived as good because it expresses his
loyalty to his child and meets the child's actual
needs. The child's value judgment that his father is
good refers to this relation. It refers at one and the
same time to the perception that his father values him
and the perception that his father meets his needs.[98]
Similarly, in religious experience, the valuation of
which we are first aware is not our own evaluation of
a being but that being's evaluation of ourselves. The
value of deity is apprehended when an object is perceived to meet loyally the structural human need for
that which makes life worth living. This primary apprehension issues in the reflexive judgment on the part
of the religious subject that this is the being of
supreme value, "which corresponds to all my deepest
needs."[99]

From this perspective, knowledge of God cannot
be founded on values accepted as absolute prior to the
religious experience of being valued by God. Since the
disclosure of the reality and value of God is fundamental, it leads to the perception that all of our
lesser relations take place within the context of this
ultimate relation. Values relative to isolated human
relations are now seen to be less than absolute. Religious experience leads people to reflect on their other
experiences in order to fashion a different vision of
the world. It leads to the criticism and reconstruction of our prior values in light of a new absolute.
The result is a transformation of ethics, rather than
support for any particular system of values accepted as
absolute prior to revelation.[100]

For Niebuhr, the task of theology is to describe
this transformation; to analyze the diverse objects
which have the value of deity for people, to show how
confidence in these objects influences their other
values and their behavior, to examine the reasons why
human confidence in the worthwhileness of life falters
when it is attached to inadequate objects, to describe
the ultimate being which alone is able to satisfy the
human need for God, and to show how the apprehension
of this sovereign Lord influences human values and
behavior.[101] Like the neo-Reformation theologians,
Niebuhr begins with revelation and tries to uphold the
integrity of faith's distinct perspective. Like the
liberals, he tries to describe intelligibly how Christian faith in God is related to the diverse loyalties
and values that emerge in ordinary life.

The critical question is whether an alternative

which tries to combine the advantages of disparate
theologies in this fashion can satisfy its own criteria. How can we make sense of the necessity of revelation without appealing to prior values? For if we
cannot make sense of this claim, then Niebuhr's proposal reduces to the Barthian insistence that revelation is without parallel in ordinary experience; and if
we can only make sense of it in light of prior values,
then his proposal reduces to another species of liberal
value-theology. The closing paragraphs of Niebuhr's
article indicate that he is aware of the difficulty.
There is, he suggests, a "remote analogy" for revelation in the "givenness" of all objects that meet the
religious need for a supreme value, and he acknowledges
that a fuller, intelligible account of the necessity
for revelation is among the cardinal requirements of
his theology.[102]

[1]KGA, p. ix.

[2]Ibid., pp. 7, 9.

[3]Ibid., p. 6.

[4]Ibid., p. 4.

[5]Ibid., p. 14.

[6]Ibid., pp. 12-13.

[7]Ibid., p. 2. See also H. Richard Niebuhr, "The Protestant Movement and Democracy in the United Sates," The Shaping of American Religion, eds. James W. Smith and A. Leland Jamison, vol. 1 Religion in American Life (Princeton: Princeton University Press, 1961), p. 26. Niebuhr's concern for the perspective of the interpreter of historical events is also evident in "Ernst Troeltsch's Philosophy of Religion," (Ph.D. Dissertation, Yale University, 1924), p. 173.

[8]KGA, p. 15.

[9]Ibid., p. 17; "The Protestant Movement and Democracy in the United States," p. 22.

[10]KGA, p. 10.

[11]Niebuhr says that dominant images influence different conceptions of individual life, the constitution of society, and the ultimate metaphysical environment. I have organized his discussion of visio dei and regnum dei in The Kingdom of God in America according to these three levels. See H. Richard Niebuhr, "The Idea of Covenant in American Democracy," Church History 23 (June 1954): 127-129.

[12]Clifford Geertz, "Religion as a Cultural System," The Interpretation of Cultures: Selected Essays (New York: Basic Books, Inc., 1973), pp. 90, 98-109. Geertz claims that religious symbols formulate general conceptions of existence clothed in an aura of factuality.

[13]KGA, pp. 19-21.

[14]Ibid., pp. 22-24.

[15]Ibid., pp. 28-29. According to Niebuhr, the Protestant Movement challenged the priestly function of the Roman Church. See H. Richard Niebuhr, "Church, the, in historic Christianity," Encyclopedia of Religion, ed. Vergilius Ferm (New York: Philosophical Library, 1945), p. 170.

[16]KGA, pp. 29-30, 32-33; "The Protestant Movement and Democracy in the United States," pp. 29-31.

[17]KGA, pp. 31-32.

[18]Ibid., pp. 33-34.

[19]Ibid., pp. 35-36. Note the similarity between this question and the relation between loyalty to God and our worldly loyalties in The Church Against the World, p. 149. Niebuhr identifies a similar relation as the problem of Christianity in Christ and Culture, p. 11. See also "The Protestant Movement and Democracy in the United States," p. 70.

[20]KGA, p. 38.

[21]Ibid., p. 39.

[22]Ibid., p. 42.

[23]"The Idea of Covenant in American Democracy," p. 131.

[24]KGA, pp. 63-64.

[25]Ibid., p. 66.

[26]Ibid., pp. 72-73.

[27]Ibid., pp. 75-76.

[28]Ibid., p. 84; "The Protestant Movement and Democracy in the United States," p. 67.

[29]KGA, pp. 83-84.

[30]Ibid., p. 102.

[31]Ibid., p. 103.

[32]Ibid., pp. 102-103.

[33]Ibid., pp. 106-107.

[34]Ibid., pp. 105, 109.

[35]Ibid., p. 109. A unitarianism of the Spirit supports early Quaker and separatist tendencies to give priority to spiritual experience over scripture. H. Richard Niebuhr, "The Doctrine of the Trinity and the Unity of the Church," Theology Today 3 (October 1946): 377.

[36]KGA, pp. 125-126.

[37]Ibid., pp. 116-117.

[38]Ibid., pp. 117-118.

[39]Ibid., p. 120.

[40]Ibid., p. 119. Niebuhr asserts that "no other awakening of love of God and neighbor compares with Edwards'" in "The Protestant Movement and Democracy in the United States," p. 35.

[41]KGA, pp. 108-109, 121-124; "The Protestant Movment and Democracy in the United States," pp. 69-70.

[42]KGA, p. 133.

[43]Ibid., p. 134.

[44]Ibid., p. 137.

[45]Ibid., p. 139. The renewal of hope during this period was not a simple revival of the expectation of immortality, but the prospect of a certain quality of life and moral freedom. See "The Protestant Movement and Democracy in the United States," pp. 32-33.

[46]KGA, pp. 140-141.

[47]Ibid., pp. 141-142.

[48]Ibid., pp. 145-147.

[49]"The Protestant Movement and Democracy in the United States," p. 58.

[50]KGA, p. 153.

[51]Ibid., pp. 187-188.

[52]Ibid., pp. 153, 155, 158.

[53] Ibid., p. 159.

[54] Ibid., p. 160.

[55] Ibid., pp. 130-131, 147-148, 186-187.

[56] Ibid, pp. 148, 160-161, 188.

[57] Ibid., pp. 20, 55, 127.

[58] Ibid., p. 165.

[59] Ibid., p. 169.

[60] Ibid., p. 173. See also H. Richard Niebuhr, "Revelation," Encyclopedia of Religion, ed. Vergilius Ferm, (New York: Philosophical Library, 1945), pp. 660-661. What Niebuhr calls "biblicism" in The Kingdom of God in America appears to correspond with the statement that the scriptures publish the content of the divine will necessary for salvation.

[61] KGA, p. 175.

[62] Ibid., p. 176.

[63] Ibid., p. 179.

[64] Ibid.

[65] Ibid., p. 181.

[66] Ibid., p. 182.

[67] Ibid., p. 183.

[68] Ibid.

[69] Ibid., p. 175.

[70] Ibid., pp. 168-169.

[71] Ibid., p. 188.

[72] Ibid., pp. 188-189.

[73] Ibid., pp. 189-190.

[74] Ibid., pp. 191-193.

[75] Ibid., p. 193.

[76]Ibid., pp. 193-194.

[77]Ibid., p. 194.

[78]Ibid.

[79]Ibid., pp. 196-197.

[80]H. Richard Niebuhr, "Value Theory and Theology," The Nature of Religious Experience: Essays in Honor of Douglas Clyde Macintosh, eds. Julius Seelye Bixler, Robert Lowry Calhoun, and H. Richard Niebuhr (New York: Harper and Brothers, 1937), pp. 93-116.

[81]Ibid., pp. 96, 107. Macintosh responded to his students in "Empirical Theology and Its Misunderstanders," The Review of Religion 3 (May 1939): 383-399; "Theology Valuational or Existential?" The Review of Religion 4 (November 1939): 23-44.

[82]"Value Theory and Theology," pp. 97, 100.

[83]Ibid., pp. 100-101.

[84]Ibid., pp. 97, 102; KGA, p. 12.

[85]"Value Theory and Theology," p. 103; CAW, p. 138.

[86]"Value Theory and Theology," p. 104.

[87]Ibid. According to Niebuhr, this criticism applies more to idealistic theologies and to the American realism of Macintosh and Wieman than to the Ritschlian school.

[88]Ibid., p. 106.

[89]Ibid., pp. 96, 107-108.

[90]Ibid., pp. 108-109.

[91]Ibid., p. 109.

[92]Ibid.

[93]Ibid., p. 110. The persistence of conflict and tragedy in human life viewed from the perspective of faith in God remains central to Niebuhr's theology and also to his critique of instrumental uses of Christianity. See "Utilitarian Christianity," p. 4.

[94] "Value Theory and Theology," p. 111.

[95] Ibid., pp. 111-112.

[96] Ibid., p. 113.

[97] H. Richard Niebuhr, "The Center of Value," RM, p. 106.

[98] "Value Theory and Theology," p. 113. Though Niebuhr does not use this example, I believe that it expresses his main point about relational value theory in this article.

[99] Ibid., p. 115.

[100] Ibid., pp. 115-116; KGA, p. 116.

[101] "Value Theory and Theology," p. 116.

[102] Ibid.

CHAPTER IV

REVELATION AND EXPERIENCE

The Meaning of Revelation offers a detailed interpretation of the relation between revelation and human experience. Though Niebuhr insists that the first value of revelation is intrinsic and that its first evidence is self-evidence, he also argues that revelation is progressively validated in the Christian life as new occasions are brought under its light. "Its success in clarifying and reconstructing souls is one source of its great prestige among us."[1] To comprehend revelation's meaning, the believer can and must order experience in light of divine reality.

Niebuhr's alternative to crisis and liberal theologies represents a delicate balance of their major interests. Like Karl Barth, he is concerned to maintain the integrity of faith in the sovereign God. This leads him to favor a confessional interpretation that guarantees the priority of revelation over human experience in theological construction. Like some liberals, however, Niebuhr is also concerned to render an intelligible account of how Christians view the world in light of revelation. This leads him to maintain that theological interpretation is comparable with other forms of discourse about the meaning of human life, and to uphold the importance of consistency or adherence to a single point of view. [2]

This second affirmation distinguishes Niebuhr's theology from that of Karl Barth, for whom the meaning of revelation is qualitatively different from the meanings of other human experiences.[3] Barth argues that since revelation does not enter human consciousness like other knowledge, it cannot be resolved into a subjective attitude or orientation.[4] Theology cannot describe a Christian view of the world that is analogous or in any way comparable with other world-views.[5] For Barth, theological interpretation, which consists exclusively in the exposition of revelation, is strictly confessional and discontinuous with other forms of discourse about the human situation.[6]

The interest in how Christians view the world is one Niebuhr shares with some liberals. Albrecht Ritschl, for example, maintains that Christian faith entails a coherent viewpoint that is analogous to and comparable with other world-views. [7] But, while Ritschl also suggests that the superiority and publicly per-

67

suasive character of the Christian viewpoint may be
demonstrated by its correspondence with universal ethical claims of the human spirit,[8] Niebuhr clearly does
not.

> To substitute the sovereignty of Christian
> religion for the sovereignty of the God of
> Christian faith, though it be done by means
> of the revelation idea, is to fall into a new
> type of idolatry, to abandon the standpoint
> of Christian faith and revelation which are
> directed toward the God of Jesus Christ and
> to take the standpoint of a faith directed
> toward religion and revelation.[9]

A public defense of Christianity departs from
faith's viewpoint because it mistakenly ascribes absolute worth to a finite thing (Christian religion) or
symbol (revelation). Faith and revelation are falsely
perverted when they do not point beyond themselves toward divine reality. Thus, the quest for a publicly
persuasive presentation of the Christian viewpoint may
develop into a misguided exercise in self-aggrandize-
ment that threatens the integrity of faith's witness to
the sovereign God.

For Niebuhr, there is room for intermediate
possibilities between the Barthian insistence that theology is credible only to believers and liberal claims
that it persuades unbelievers of the validity of Christianity by demonstrating the agreement of Christian
faith with cultural norms and standards. His mediating
position is that theology may interpret Christian faith
and revelation so that they are convincing to believers
and understandable to others. For Niebuhr, however,
understanding is not the same thing as agreement. One
may understand how an individual arrives at a particular
judgment and still believe that his judgment is mis-
taken. To claim that a viewpoint is understandable to
persons who do not subscribe to it is not the same
thing as to claim that it makes no sense to others or
that others implicity agree with it. According to
Niebuhr, intelligible theological statements are convincing to believers and understandable to unbelievers.
This is all the public status possible for theological
statements as well as all the status that is necessary.

Clearly, this mediating alternative invites
criticism from both quarters. For liberals, Niebuhr's
reliance on special revelation borders upon obscurant-
ism. Barthians will insist that all attempts at media-

tion compromise the integrity of faith in God by determining revelation in light of human experience and
standards of judgment. The proposed balance is threatened on the one hand by liberal apologists who reduce
the essentials of faith to harmony with the dominant
views of culture. On the other hand, the tendency of
crisis theology to disparage reason and divorce revelation from experience threatens to reduce faith to the
unintelligible assertion of transcendent reality.

In order to meet these challenges, Niebuhr
suggests a complex series of arguments. Against the
liberal camp, he maintains that efforts to defend the
validity of Christianity to unbelievers are inconsistent with the viewpoint of faith, and that theology is
forced to be confessional on epistemological as well as
specifically religious grounds. If these assertions
are defensible, his confessional reliance on revelation
is neither obscure nor esoteric. Against the objections of the Barthians, he argues that a skeptical regard for reason and experience is unwarranted, and that
theology is required to construct a comprehensive view
of God, creation, and humanity for specifically Christian as well as more general reasons. If these arguments are successful, the Barthian insistence that
revelation be radically separated from reason and experience loses its sting.

Revelation and Experience

The modern realization that non-logical elements influence thinking, that what we experience is
qualified by our psychological equipment and the historical inheritance of our particular society, threatens
to dissolve knowledge into subjectivism.[10] Since a
skeptical estimate of the reliability of thought leads
inexorably to the separation of revelation from reason
and experience, it would appear that the intelligibility of theological claims is in a quandary. But Niebuhr
does not believe this is the case. In order to avoid
the separation of revelation from experience and defend
his position against charges that the reliance on special revelation is esoteric, he argues that theology is
forced to begin with revelation precisely because revelation founds a distinctive historical viewpoint.

According to Niebuhr, we are aware of different basic knowing relations. Knowledge gained through
the relation of a knowing subject to a passive object
differs from knowledge gained through the relation of
a self to other selves.[11] Whereas the impersonal

observer tries to discover what is the case about things and persons considered as objects external to his self-understanding, personal knowing involves a complex interaction between purposive and intentional selves. Here, the other is an agent or community of agents who are integral to the knower's self-understanding and identity. The involved participant tries to discern how to respond appropriately to other selves.[12]

People are typically involved in knowing relations of both kinds. For Niebuhr, "no man in the situation of a participant in life" succeeds in dealing with others exclusively on the impersonal level.[13] The psychologist who devotes his work-day to stimulus-response experiments with human subjects continues to regard his family as centered, unified, and responsible selves. He cannot effectively deal with his family "on the hypothesis that there is no consciousness of self but only an impersonal process of mind or matter."[14]

Surely, there are important connections between impersonal and personal knowing. The psychologist who holds his children responsible for their actions may also be aware of reasons why they act as they do. Nevertheless, says Niebuhr, two important levels of judgment may be distinguished.

For Niebuhr, Christian tradition has understood revelation as the self-disclosure of God through the medium of a person in Jesus Christ.[15] Theology is, therefore, primarily and immediately concerned with our interpersonal knowledge of selves rather than our contemplative knowledge of things.[16] Thus, one qualification placed on religious and theological judgments is that they are not of the same sort as judgments about impersonal realities.

Even on the level of personal knowing, however, the actions and intentions of selves carry different meanings in different social and historical contexts. What once were thought to be self-evident truths or ideals in relations among persons now appear as notions of value deeply imbedded in our historically and socially conditioned experience.[17] There is no universal thought or idea evident to all persons in all places at all times, but only ideas that are meaningful and valuable for persons who share the same basic viewpoint. The recognition that our reasoning about personal relations is relative to our social and historical background adds a perspectival dimension to the knowing process.[18] The Christian viewpoint is a particular perspective on the level of personal knowing.

At this point, it appears that Niebuhr has established the very skepticism he wished to avoid. For, if religious knowledge is a species of personal knowing, and if personal knowing is relative to an individual's social and historical perspective, why should we trust theology as anything other than a collection of subjective opinions? But this misses the major point of Niebuhr's argument. His position is not that reality is communicated to individuals in spite of conditioning factors, but rather that reality is mediated to individuals through psychologically and historically conditioned experience.

For Niebuhr, basic questions concerning the reliability and meaning of personal knowledge are deeper than reason. They are questions of faith.[19] Whatever doubts people may have about the reliability of thought, they trust their perceptions. This trust or "animal faith" entails the basic belief that an external world or independent reality exists to which our perceptions ultimately refer.[20] Though this belief does not have the same status as a perception and is not logically demonstrable, it is pragmatically justifiable because persons could not successfully engage in their various activities without it. It is a virtually necessary and, therefore, reasonable inference from our basic trust in our perceptions.

Like William James, however, Niebuhr maintains that individuals are not merely passive recipients of experiential impressions. The primitive richness of experience needs to be broken down, sorted, and refined if it is to be intelligently appropriated by finite minds.[21] Individuals engage in this sorting process with the aid of imaginative symbols and images which they apply to their perceptions. In addition to simple perception, then, knowing involves a continuous exchange between perception and imagination.[22]

A professor, for example, uses an image of what it means to be a student in order to refer to particular persons. He is aware that each person is a complex individual, and at times other dimensions of the student's life may be brought to his attention. His continued experience of students may even lead him to adjust or modify his image. Nevertheless, the professor employs his imaginative notion of what it means to be a student in order to focus his attention on a single, limited aspect of an individual's personal reality. Moreover, though the professor's image of what it means to be a student may be distinctive, it did not originate with him. He has internalized the image through participation in a community of learning. The imaginative patterns or images persons use to refine their experience are acquired socially.

The professor's internalized image or notion of what it means to be a student is part of his remembered past that functions as a selective instrument for his interpretation of experienced reality and guides his behavior as a teacher. In the course of its application, he may discern that the image enables him to select a portion of experience as particularly significant and worthy of being known because it implies and is accompanied by an underlying conviction or value orientation. The wider interpretative framework that involves the notion of what it means to be a student, a professor, and so on, reflects a commitment to the value and importance of learning held in common by members of an educational community. The professor is able to focus his attention on a limited aspect of an individual's personal reality because he shares the estimate of his community that learning is worthy of special attention.

For Niebuhr, the interpreted experience is neither purely subjective nor purely objective. Though reality in itself is not directly available, interpreted experience represents a combination of imaginative patterns or constructs with reality. It is a middle term or medium that stands between subjective consciousness (imagination) and objective reality. The imaginative patterns or images that people employ enable them to view reality in a particular way.

When the professor trusts his ordered interpretation or knowledge of students, then, he has a kind of "social faith" or confidence in the reliability of his acquired interpretative perspective and its standard of judgment. He believes that images of what it means to be a student, a professor, and so on "fit" with important aspects of reality. Moreover, this social faith in the significance of learning which affirms the meaningfulness of the professor's involvement in teaching implies the further belief that something of reality is mediated to individuals through their social perspectives. The professor's social faith is the further development of his animal faith in an external world for it allows him to order his experience in terms of particular images and patterns of interaction.[23]

According to Niebuhr, an individual's social belief may be partially justified if it is subject to intersubjective confirmation. The professor can check his interpretation of students with the interpretations of his colleagues. If he finds that their interpreted experience is similar to his own, his experience accumulates the force or authority of intersubjectivity. His experience is not entirely discrete or private. Instead, it is an experience he holds in common with social companions who share a view of reality.

In the case that his interpretation of a particular student differs from that of another faculty member, they may appeal to other features of their common experience of the student in question or to the judgments of other faculty. If fundamental disagreement persists, eventually they may appeal to a standard for judgment which they hold in common that defines the responsibilities of students for clarification. In this way, intersubjective confirmation and the norm or standard of judgment in a community restrain the uncritical exercise of subjective evaluation and cooperatively direct the attention and judgments of many individuals.

Though these checks certify important features of reliable knowledge, the realization that there are many people who do not share a community's judgments may raise further questions about the reliability of their common perspective. Professors may notice, for example, that significant numbers of people do not share their estimate of the importance of learning. When such basic questions arise concerning a community's standard of judgment, it becomes apparent that though their experience of reality may be intersubjective, it is something less than universally available.

Should people in this situation persist in believing that something of the reality of persons is mediated through their perspective, it becomes possible to state their social belief more precisely. They now understand that their point of view is relative and conditioned. Their persistent belief is that some significant aspect of the fuller, complex reality of persons is mediated to them through their relative and conditioned perspective. Justification of this belief requires that something be said about the way intersubjective perspectives come into being.

Niebuhr resists the conclusion that knowledge is no more than a mutual agreement among members of a specific community by the insistence that perspectives themselves arise in response to experienced realities.[24] Special experiences or encounters with reality have an unusual force or power. They impose their own interpretative categories and demand consideration in their own terms, because they touch our lives at some basic level and elicit a fundamental commitment or value judgment. Consequently, these experiences or events provide individuals with distinct, paradigmatic images and symbols for their interpretations of other experiences.

To return to our example, professors who call the reliability of their perspective into question may find that they have had some formative experience which impressed them with the importance and value of learning. This experience may have intensely personal dimensions, but it is also one that they share with others in their community. Perhaps they will find that their long apprenticeships in communities of learning constitute such an experience for them, and that this experience cast up images of what it means to be a student, a professor, and so on. Furthermore, they may find that the meaning of this experience has been progressively deepened, refined and clarified by their subsequent experience as teachers. Beyond an appeal to this special shared experience or occasion, however, no further justification of the reliability of their perspective is possible. There comes a point in personal discourse and reasoning beyond which we cannot go without circling back to where we began. At this point, decision is king.

In the Christian community, revelation in Jesus Christ is the special experience beyond which no further justificatory appeal is possible. It constitutes the believer's first certainty because it elicits a faith commitment to the significance or value of divine reality in light of which the believer applies interpretative images to his experiences. Though this special experience has intensely personal dimensions, revelation is not an exclusively private experience. Its unusual force or power may distinguish it from other experiences, but it is not an immediate, mystical apprehension of reality. Rather, revelation is the special, intersubjective and historically mediated experience of divine reality that touches the lives of believers at a basic level and casts up images of what it means to be human in relation to God.

74

Revelation in History

What is revealed or manifested to the church
at this preconceptual, imaginative level, says Niebuhr,
can only be indicated by recalling an especially forma-[25]
tive experience or event in the life of the community.
Thus, revelational theology begins with the preconceptual inspiration for dogma rather than refined theological propositions. [26] It begins with a confessional remembrance of special events. According to Niebuhr,
this starting point parallels the proclamation of the
early church which "was primarily a simple recital of
the great events connected with the historical appear-
ance of Jesus Christ and a confession of what happened
to the community of disciples."[27]

The emphasis on revelation in history recovers
an explicitly theological dimension of the Bible and
asserts its relevance for modern Christians.[28] As
examples of "the historical method" of speaking about
revelation, Niebuhr quotes the Pauline kerygma in I
Corinthians 15 and mentions the sermon at Antioch in
Acts and the prologue to John's gospel.[29] But this
emphasis also raises a notorious problem. If the same
historical events may be regarded by unbelievers as
quite ordinary occurrences, what is the precise relation between revelation and history?

What believers mean by revelation, says Niebuhr,
can only be indicated through the historical and social
medium in which they live.[30] Consequently, if scripture is to point toward God, it must be interpreted
through the perspective of Christian faith and history.
The Bible may be read in a variety of contexts from
different points of view, but only when it is read
through the spectacles of faith and in the context
of the Christian community can it be understood as
revelation.

Thus, history understood as revelation depends
upon a circular process of interpretation. Historical
events which are already "memorable" with the aid of
monuments and records become the story of a community's
life when they are viewed through the very interpretative spectacles that have grown out of the shared
past.[31] The story of a community's life which emerges
from this process is a personal, value-laden history
that has to do with the identity and self-understanding
of selves. Individuals who participate in the life of
the community locate and identify themselves in terms
of its interpreted history.[32]

Niebuhr refers to this personal, value-laden history as "internal history" and contrasts it with the "external history" of observers.[33] Clearly, the same events held dear by persons who participate in a community's life may be regarded differently from an external point of view. As an example, Niebuhr notes the difference between descriptions of the American Revolution offered by Abraham Lincoln in his Gettysburg Address and the authors of the Cambridge Modern History.[34]

The critical point is that events may be significant in different ways. Some events have the capacity to shape the preconceptual imaginative foundations for our interpretations of other experiences and events. They become significant for a community of selves at the level of personal knowing. Consequently, they recommend themselves to social memory, and the community preserves their meaning in stories and recitals.

In order to understand and grasp an occurrence as a revelatory event, one must view it in the context of the communal history of which it is a part from an internal, participatory perspective. The appeal to revelation in history then does not mean that believers appeal to events which unbelievers are unable to reconstruct as historical occurrences.

The difference between the believer and the unbeliever is not whether a given event occurred; rather, the difference lies in the way the event is interpreted, the significance attributed to the event. This difference in perspective may be such that the two descriptions of the same event differ, but the two descriptions are not incompatible in the way that two differing claims over whether it happened or not are incompatible.[35]

As we have seen, the origin of a perspective and its standard of judgment can finally be explained only with reference to a special event of such force that it shapes or alters our imaginative framework for interpretation in a fundamental way. The origin of the Christian perspective and its norm or standard of judgment constitutes the christological problem.[36] But a confessional reliance on a special historical event is neither esoteric nor obscure since the same problem is present in all other perspectives. To return to the earlier example, the perspective of a community of learning is based in some shared experience that provides a standard of value and judgment and provides people with interpretative images. Similarly, the perspectives of national communities are based in standards of judgment that emerge from specially formative events.[37]

Against the challenge of liberal theology, Niebuhr's perspectivism suggests that the conditioned nature of the general knowing process requires a crit[38] ical historical theology that begins with revelation. Precisely because questions concerning the reliability of knowledge and experience finally demand that persons recall the meaning and significance of some particular event, the logical starting point for theological inquiry must be that special event. Thus, a theology that is consistent with the conditioned nature of historical knowledge gives up all pretensions to a universally persuasive starting point. It begins with revelation because revelation furnishes believers with a new imaginative basis for value-laden interpretation of their experience.

Furthermore, Niebuhr's epistemological reflections suggest that _in fact_ we do not believe our experiences and thoughts are unreliable vehicles for knowledge of reality. The realization that our knowledge is psychologically and historically qualified demands that we realize the profound importance of the point of view a man occupies in regarding reality.[39] But it does not require the dissolution of knowledge into subjectivism. "It is not evident that the man who is forced to confess that his view of things is conditioned by the standpoint he occupies must doubt the reality of what he sees."[40]

Against the objections of crisis theologians, this conclusion enables Niebuhr to maintain that revelation need not be separated from experience in order to free knowledge of God from subjectivity and unreliability. Instead, when faith in God is understood as a distinct variety of "social faith," it becomes apparent that Christian faith itself entails the belief that something of the absolute, sovereign God is mediated to believers _through_ the interpretative images cast up by the conditioned, historic experience of the Christian community.

One consequence of Niebuhr's position is that the believer's conditioned perspective affords only a partial apprehension of divine reality. But, just as the man who is forced to confess the relative and conditioned nature of his viewpoint need not doubt the reality of what he sees, Christian believers need not doubt the reality of God mediated to them through their relative conditioned experience. Mature faith can assert that there is a God, though all our knowledge is but a poor and imperfect approximation of his reality.

Finally, Niebuhr's understanding of the origin of interpretative perspectives implies that the sovereignty or independence of God is not negated or qualified by the close association of revelation with historic experience. Not only does revelation cast up distinct images which shape the believer's interpretations, but the vivid revelatory experience and the application of these images to experience give rise to a new faith commitment and standard of judgment. This is the crucial importance of Niebuhr's insistence that the judgment that God is the reality of supreme value is a reflexive judgment elicited by God's revelatory self-disclosure.[41] The believer's standard of judgment is his response to revelation rather than the precondition for revelation.

Niebuhr's theology is confessional in the sense that it begins with the event that founds the Christian viewpoint. This guards the integrity of faith. There is no reason to assume either that unbelievers will understand the special significance of the revelatory event and the shared recitals in the same way believers do, or that they will necessarily find interpretations of experiences and events in light of this special experience convincing. At the same time, to begin with revelation is an intelligible procedure precisely because it is consistent with the conditioned nature of historical knowledge and analogous to the starting-points of other social perspectives. The theologian expects unbelievers to understand why he begins with the revelatory event and recitals. He does not expect unbelievers to comprehend fully the significance of these primary "facts" for theology.

Thus, if the author of The Kingdom of God in America suggested that the historian of American Protestantism provisionally adopt the standpoint of its fundamental faith in God's reign,[42] the author of The Meaning of Revelation argues that the theologian who would see divine reality and human life as Christians see it must share the faith and viewpoint of the Christian community. This places stringent limitations

78

on Christian theology. It cannot abandon the Christian perspective in order to view things apart from their explicit, beliefully realistic reference to divine reality.

> Christian theology must begin today with reve-
> lation because it knows that men cannot think
> about God save as historic, communal beings
> and save as believers. It must ask what reve-
> lation means for Christians rather than what
> it ought to mean for all men at all times. And
> it can pursue its inquiry only by recalling the
> story of Christian life and by analyzing what
> Christians see from their limited point of view
> in history and faith.[43]

In sum, theology is forced to begin within the historic experience of the Christian community because of the sovereign nature of divine reality and because of the perspectival character of knowledge. It is required to be a revelational theology for general epistemological reasons as well as specifically religious reasons.[44] It is, therefore, constrained to begin where the early Christian communities began: with a confessional recital of the irreplaceable and untranslatable events that have happened to believers.[45]

The Reinterpretation of Experience

For Niebuhr, Jesus Christ is the irreplaceable event in whom Christians encounter the reality of God and a suggestion of what it means to live in relation to that reality. The decisive occasion preserved in confessional recitals elicits an affective sense of divine presence and includes the reflexive value judgment on the part of believers that God is the most important reality with which persons have to deal. Christians believe in order to understand or, more precisely, they believe in order to interpret.

The disclosure of the sovereign Lord demands that all things be understood in a beliefully realistic fashion, in light of their explicit reference to divine reality. Christian faith involves an active believing that relates all things appropriately to God.[46] The believer cannot remain content with the initial strange warming of the heart, but must endeavor to construct a comprehensive vision of reality on the basis of revelation. In this sense, revelation is the "intelligible event which makes all other events intelligible."[47] The believer uses this special experience to order his other experiences in the world.

Niebuhr's often-cited definition of revelation informs his conception of theological interpretation and implicitly rejects the strict confessionalism of the crisis theologians. For Niebuhr, the sovereignty of God entails his universality, and for this reason the Christian community is required "to regard all events . . . as the workings of the one sovereign God."[48] Consequently, revelation requires that believers construct a world view in order to understand their faith.

Religious thoughts and sensibilities arise when the imaginative pattern of the special occasion is fitted with other occasions. They are inferred as the revelatory image is applied as an interpretative key to experience. Believers appeal to a special occasion and to the elucidatory power of concepts inferred from it for all occasions.[49] Thus, religious sensibilities have a dual referent. They refer to the vivid encounter with divine reality and to the interpretative application of the patterns cast up by this encounter to other experiences and events.

It should be noted, however, that this is a largely intuitive process that is not strictly logical. It is as incorrect to say that the believer's religious sensibilities are inductive generalizations on the basis of experience as it is to suppose that they represent simple deductions from some divinely communicated cardinal principle or proposition. Rather, they are inferences from the dispositions of the heart which emerge as the explanatory capabilities of the encounter with divine reality are displayed in relation to the facts of experience.[50] Throughout this loose inferential process, the believer's initial sense of divine presence is deepened while religious apprehensions of the world and the Christian viewpoint are progressively refined.[51]

Without the aid of revelation, says Niebuhr, individuals typically interpret their experience with the aid of an image of the self as protagonist.[52] Coupled with a disposition toward or interest in the self's welfare and security, this image directs the attention of the interpreting agent. The human situation is interpreted by an egoistic faith and vision. All things are construed in terms of their relation to the self.

A reinterpretation of experience becomes possible when this self-interested center for interpretation is replaced by a sense of divine presence and the christological image. It is important to emphasize that revelation does not furnish the individual with a new vision, but holds forth the possibility of a new perspective. It does not obviate the necessity of practical reasoning, but rather enables individuals to reinterpret their experience on the basis of a different imaginative pattern. When the self reasons about its experience on the basis of revelation, a new dramatic pattern of unity begins to emerge.[53]

Reinterpretation of experience under the influence of revelation involves individuals in the reconstruction of their identities. On the basis of revelation, individuals begin to understand their remembered pasts in accordance with a new point of reference.

In the life of an individual a great occasion may make significant and intelligible the apparently haphazard course of his earlier existence; all that has happened to him may then assume continuity and pattern as it is related to the moment for which he knows himself to have been born.[54]

Augustine's Confessions is a classic example. The bishop of Hippo interprets his early studies in rhetoric along with his fascination with Manichees and Platonists as stepping stones on the road to his conversion at Milan. In short, he is both enabled and impelled to construe his personal history as an autobiography centered around the special event that discloses supremely valuable reality to him.

A similar point can be made about communities. Special occasions that bind individuals together and mold their perspectives become "centers of history" around which communities focus their visions. "So the Scriptures were written not as the history of revelation only but as the history of Israel understood and unified by means of revelation."[55] In the Christian community, says Niebuhr, the function of revelation in Jesus Christ has been similar. Through this central event, the Christian community makes all memories its own. The church appropriates and interprets the moral codes of Gentile Christians, the shrill voices of Hebrew prophets, the faith of Abraham, and the sin of Adam as its own memory through Jesus Christ. "There is no part of the past that can be ignored or regarded as beyond the possibility of redemption from meaninglessness."[56]

Consequently, revelation also drives individuals and communities to remember what their fragmented self-interested visions have repressed. It "demands and permits that we bring into the light of attention our betrayals and denials, our follies and our sins."[57] Since the self-interested image is no longer the center of interpretation, revelation allows transgressions to be brought to light without jeopardizing the center of meaning and value. Revelation enables the construction of a critical history of self and community.[58]

According to Niebuhr, the life and death of Christ may also be used as a parable and analogy to interpret present experience. The story of Jesus, and particularly of his passion, is the great illustration that enables us to say, "What we are now doing and suffering is like this."[59] Through the use of the great parable, Christians are able to recognize betrayals and denials that take place in the present. They discern, however dimly, a pattern of divine action amidst the confusion of contemporary experience.

The most vivid application of the revelatory pattern to experience in Niebuhr's published work is "War As Crucifixion."[60] In this short article, Niebuhr argues that "amoral" theories which interpret war as the simple clash of raw power and "moral" theories that interpret war as "an event in a universe in which the laws of retribution hold sway" are both inadequate to "the facts of experience." Amoral theories fail to account for the curious mixture of lofty self-sacrifice and blatant self-interest that characterizes the motives of fighting men on both sides. Moral theories (which are usually the ideologies of the victors) ignore the fact that suffering falls on the innocent even more than the guilty.

Niebuhr suggests that the revelatory pattern places war in the context of the world governed by the sovereign God. This wider context enables a more realistic assessment of the facts of experience. Through the interpretative spectacles of the revelatory image, it is plain that "retribution for the sins of a Nazi party and a Hitler falls on Russian and German soldiers, on the children of Cologne and Coventry, on the Finns and the French."[61]

There are a number of similarities between war

and the crucifixion. In both, justice is confused, and justice confused with injustice is "apparently indiscriminate in the choice of victims and victors."[62] The cross does not encourage moral indifference or despair. It calls upon people to take their moral decisions with greater seriousness because it reveals the moral earnestness of a God who will not abandon his creation to perverted self-destruction. Like the sacrifices of soldiers, the crucifixion

> does all this because it is sacrifice--the self-sacrifice of Jesus Christ for the sake of the just and the unjust. War is like the cross in this respect. In its presence men must abandon their moral cynicism along with other peacetime luxuries.[63]

The interpretation of war through the image of crucifixion lays bare a fundamental pattern of self-sacrifice. It identifies sensitivities and hopes which inform the believer's interpretation of experience and his response to it. In the midst of suffering, the Christian who looks through the revelatory pattern partly senses and partly hopes that God refuses to abandon his creation to suffering and death. The Christian reinterpretation of experience and history "centers in the conviction that God is at work in all events" and its ethic is "determined by the principle that man's action ought always to be response to divine rather than finite action."[64] The attention of the believer is directed to the suffering and death of the guiltless as a self-giving sacrifice and call to repentance.[65]

As believers interpret war with the aid of the revelatory image, it becomes apparent that the cross not only illumines the present situation, but contemporary experience also contributes to the meaning of the cross. Believers are able to discern the meaning of the great sacrifice with greater clarity through the tragic sacrifices of fighting men. "The analogy of war and crucifixion suggests that we are dealing with more than an analogy."[66] Indeed, if Jesus Christ is not only a historical event and a person but also a revelation of the order of reality, then present experience is not only like Jesus Christ; it is a demonstration of that same order of God.[67]

Niebuhr's articles on the War interpret present experience in light of divine judgment and crucifixion.[68] To begin with these events recounted in biblical recitals is to guard the integrity of faith's perspective, to insist that faith's vision account for these "facts" of the Christian heritage. But to apply these events as elucidatory symbols in present experience is also to anticipate the affirmation that they disclose an intelligible pattern, and to adopt the hypothesis "that there is no event in which divine reason and will are not involved."[69] In short, to reinterpret particular events (the War) in light of particular events (the recitals) is to affirm that the universal God is only present in the particular. This is the philosophical meaning of the statement that God acts in particular events, and it impels the believer "to discover the universal in every particular and respond to it."[70]

The examples of critical autobiography, communal history, and war viewed through the crucifixion indicate that the reinterpretation of experience in light of revelation is at least partly the work of creative imagination. Niebuhr's short essay shows that there are few hard and fast rules for the appropriate apprehension of an interpretative analogy. Creative imagination apprehends broad similarities between a fact of experience and an image in the biblcal witness. It selects an image from the constellation of patterns and images cast up by revelation as its guiding interpretative lens. This is one reason why classics of religious literature like Augustine's Confessions or The City of God are regarded as significant creative achievements.

Even so, there appear to be some general guidelines for the reinterpretation of experience from Niebuhr's perspective. Religious sensibilities and concepts emerge as images cast up by revelation are "fitted" with ordinary experience. This reinterpretation is guided and controlled by the historical revelation which founds the Christian viewpoint. The redescription of experience through the use of revelation as parable and analogy forms the primary level of religious speech. This discourse is a virtually preconceptual, literary language that displays the elucidatory capabilities of the encounter with divine reality at the basic level of life in the world lived in conscious relation to God. It is faith seeking understanding at the most fundamental level, the basic language of preaching and religious sensibility that embodies and conveys the illuminative relation between the special experience of divine reality and the rest of life.[71] To the extent that this speech is controlled by the particular historic images of revelation, it is faithful to the distinctive features of the biblical witness. To the extent that it successfully interprets and orders lived experience in a coherent pattern, this first order religious discourse offers an intelligible redescription of human life.

The redescription of experience precipitates a transformation of life and its fervent loyalties. Augustine's autobiographical reassessment underscores the seriousness of youthful thievery and the superficiality of a life centered around rhetorical accomplishments. His redescription of the ancient republic betrays the nobility of Roman gloria in light of a loyalty to the heavenly city. In Niebuhr's redescription of the Second World War, the earnestness of self-sacrifice displaces the motives of nationalistic pride and moralistic retribution.[72]

Theology takes up the suggestion of first order discourse that Jesus Christ is more than an analogy. It goes beyond the first order reinterpretation in order to describe recurrent features of experience in relation to God. General concepts are inferred on the basis of first order discourse so that beyond interpretations of what particular life-times, communities, and events are like, theology may suggest a more comprehensive and general vision of divine action and human response. In short, theology tries to elucidate the universal claim of Christian faith that Jesus Christ is the logos made flesh by suggesting that our actions and sufferings interpreted with the aid of revelation indicate something about the order of God's world in which we live and move.

The inference of theological concepts involves a secondary, more abstract level of meaning and language. One of the functions of theological discourse is to provide believers with highly general notions of what to expect in their converse with mundane reality governed by the universal and sovereign God. The theologian tries to help believers order and reflect upon their lived experience in accordance with a consistent, rationalized or systematized pattern of doctrine. Though traditional records of what has happened in the past are helpful, they do not obviate the necessity of normative maps or guidelines for Christian life in converse with the living and present Lord. Theology furnishes believers with general concepts that enable the construction of a comprehensive and beliefully realistic vision of the ultimate context for human life. Its usefulness is in its provision of an interpretative pattern of meaning and value for life and experience in God's world.

The development of this vision is both informed and controlled by revelation to the extent that the pattern of particular historical events disclosive of divine reality forms the basis for the religious sensibilities for life and experience that theology seeks to extend and clarify. At the same time, a concern for intelligibility is evident in the effort to provide an interpretative vision capable of elucidating wide areas of human experience.

For Niebuhr, the use of second order theological discourse always involves the temptation to identify the meaning and value of revelation with abstract principles and ideas. In the service of a more refined and rationalized understanding of human life in relation to God, theology risks the reification and distortion of the lived experience of divine reality. Consequently, he believes that theology should re-check and revise its abstract conceptualizations in accordance with the unique, unrepetitive pattern of the revelatory event and the first order application of this pattern to lived experience.

It follows that, to ensure the fidelity of theology to the historic features of biblical revelation, the theologian ought to re-check his preliminary and provisional articulation of a theological vision against the biblical sources. "Concepts and doctrines derived from the unique historical moment are important but less illuminating than the occasion itself."[73] It also follows that adequacy to lived experience in God's world takes priority over the requirements of formal logical consistency in the development of a more or less comprehensive presentation of doctrine. Theological discourse is irretrievably tied to the elucidatory power of the revelatory event and the first order discourse of religious sensibilities.

On the other hand, the language of religious sensibility and the language of theology seek intelligibility for theological as well as more general reasons. The unity of God and his universality as the personal will active in all creation and in redemption require that the believer both discern and respond to all events as the actions of the sovereign Lord. Faith's apprehension of the unity and universality of God impels the language of religious sensibility to interpret life experiences that are common to others and not peculiar to Christian believers. This discourse enters the public marketplace of competing viewpoints when it undertakes an interpretation of the common experiences of family life or the public events of the Second World War. Since the facts of family life and the Second World War are not different for Christians than for non-Christians, a religious interpretation of these experiences that is persuasive to believers ought at least to be understandable to those outside the Christian community.

Theological discourse goes beyond the limits of the strictly confessional apprehension of divine reality almost by definition. By offering interpretations of the order of experience and the world in relation to God, it necessarily enters the public marketplace of general interpretations of human life offered by non-Christian philosophies and other religions. In order to elucidate the sense of divine unity and universality, this more conceptual language offers interpretations of the general character of history, the world, and human life. To help guide and interpret the lives of believers who participate in the world, theology compares its vision with the interpretations of human experience offered by other religions and other disciplines, showing where it is similar and where it differs from other views.

In addition to faith's apprehension of the sovereignty and universality of God, then, the theologian has a practical and pastoral motive for constructing a comprehensive and intelligible vision. Believers who participate in God's world cannot interpret their own experience and history in light of revelation without discussing experiences and events that are part of the public domain. This is the case whenever Christians interpret regular features of ordinary experience like marriage and family life, historical events whose significance is not confined to the Christian community like the Second World War, and conditions of general human life like dependence on others, freedom, and responsibility. The fact that much of what believers experience and are compelled to interpret is also experienced and interpreted by non-believers provides a general warrant for going beyond strict confessionalism.

To summarize, the religious reinterpretation of life in light of revelation proceeds in accordance with the requirements of integrity and intelligibility at the level of religious sensibility and explicitly theological concepts. This is so for specifically re-

ligious as well as more general reasons. Revelation
takes priority in the development of a theological vision due to the conviction of divine sovereignty and
also because of the requirements of human knowing in
history and society. Conversely, the universality and
power of God as well as the general character of important features of the believer's experience require that
this theological vision seek an intelligible and comprehensive interpretation of human life.

An important implication of the criterion of
intelligibility is that theology enters the public
marketplace of interpretations of human life and experience. This means it makes a number of different
claims. Theological claims about the meaning of human
life entail assertions about experience, e.g., "Some
experiences in the world have the pattern of self-
sacrifice." These claims are cognitive or theoretical.
But theological redescription also recommends certain
patterns and courses of action, e.g., "Respond to all
events as actions of the sovereign God." These claims
are practical or moral.

Niebuhr's resolution to the question of revelation and experience allows for the diverse practical
and theoretical claims made by religious sensibilities
and doctrines. According to Niebuhr, theological assertions about God and human experience give the believer a distinct reason to care about his actions.
The world is now construed as a whole unified by its
relation to a single divine agent and his purposes.[74]
One ought to be moral because one meets the intention
and purposes of the sovereign and good God in all
events. Moreover, since all persons and things are
now seen to have value in virtue of their relation to
God and the total process producing good, Niebuhr's
theological vision recommends a pattern of universal
responsibility for moral life. No person or thing,
whether or not it contributes to the good as people
ordinarily conceive it apart from revelation, is without value. The believer is impelled to respond to all
creation as deserving of fitting moral reply.

Niebuhr's discussions of relations between inner and outer history indicate that theological interpretation also involves cognitive claims that impinge
on other fields of inquiry and discourse.[75] The claim
that Jesus Christ is the Son of the living Lord is connected with historical claims about his life, ministry,
and death. A theological interpretation of the Second
World War clearly involves claims about historical

matters of fact. Similarly, a theological statement about the texture and meaning of human life may be connected with certain psychological, social scientific, and even biological claims. As Niebuhr understands it, the principle of intelligibility requires that theological interpretation sometimes admit the relevance of principles of judgment drawn from other disciplines and realms of discourse.

But theological claims are not identical with the logically diverse claims with which they are connected. Major theological doctrines offer distinct redescriptions of the facts of history, human life, and experience. While the theological assertion that Jesus Christ is the Son of God is connected with historical claims, it is not reducible to historical claims. Similarly, though Niebuhr's interpretation of the Second World War depends on certain historical claims, e.g., that Russians, Finns, and French die in the war, his claims about the pattern of self-sacrifice in the war and its force as a call to repentance cannot be reduced to historical claims. Christian theology interprets facts of human life and experience in relation to the God disclosed in and through special experiences. This redescription transforms our value-laden visions of what it means to be human in relation to the power active in all things. Revelation is the special principle of judgment in theology, and the criterion of integrity means that revelation takes priority over relevant principles of judgment drawn from other fields of inquiry and discourse.76

One of Niebuhr's important insights is to see that while the reception of revelation does not require any single social faith or background, no one comes to revelation without some prior social faith and interpretative vision. Indeed, the biblical witnesses themselves did not come to revelation without the social faiths of their Hebrew and Hellenistic cultures and the social achievement of the church. Since the reality of God is necessarily mediated to people through their social and historical experience, Christians are left to adjudicate the relation between their faith in God and their faith in the cultural perspective through which revelation in Christ has been mediated to them. Transformationism is one way to adjudicate this relation, but there are others. Resolutions to this problem are basic to theology since they support different estimates of the relation between revelation and experience, different specifications of integrity and intelligibility, and different understandings of Christian ethics.

[1]MR, pp. 97-98.

[2]Ibid., pp. xxi. Niebuhr tried to combine the main interests of Karl Barth and Ernst Troeltsch. Barth criticized all such attempts at mediation. See Karl Barth, CD, 2/1:214.

[3]Barth, CD, 2/1:259.

[4]Ibid., 2/1:73.

[5]Ibid., 1/1:207-217; 2/1:63.

[6]Ibid., 2/1:203, 212.

[7]Albrecht Ritschl, The Christian Doctrine of Justification and Reconciliation, eds. H.R. Mackintosh and A.B. Macaulay, trans. A.B. Macaulay et al. (Clifton, New Jersey: Reference Book Publishers, 1966), p. 24.

[8]Ibid., pp. 8, 10, 13, 25, 609-612. See also MR, pp. 21-24. A similar justification is also important for dogmatics according to Ernst Troeltsch. See Ernst Troeltsch, "The Dogmatics of the 'Religion-geschichte Schule,'" American Journal of Theology 17 (January 1913): 121. See also Brian A. Gerrish, "The Possibility of a Historical Theology," Ernst Troeltsch and the Future of Theology, ed. John Powell Clayton (Cambridge: Cambridge University Press, 1976), pp. 105-106.

[9]MR, p. 29.

[10]Ibid., pp. 12-13.

[11]Ibid., pp. 49-52, 75.

[12]Donald E. Fadner, The Responsible God: A Study of the Christian Philosophy of H. Richard Niebuhr, American Academy of Religion Dissertation Series, no. 13 (Missoula, Montana: Scholars Press, 1975), pp. 81-96.

[13]MR, p. 76.

[14]Ibid., pp. 77.

[15]Ibid., pp. 101-114.

[16]Ibid., pp. 49-52, 56, 75. See also RS, pp. 108-126.

[17]MR, pp. 7-10.

[18]H. Richard Niebuhr, "Faith in Gods and in God," RM, p. 115.

[19]H. Richard Niebuhr, "Life Is Worth Living," The Intercollegian and Far Horizon 57 (October 1939): 34.

[20]Ibid.; MR, pp. 14, 58.

[21]See William James, Essays in Radical Empiricism and a Pluralistic Universe, ed. Ralph Barton Perry (New York: E. P. Dutton Company, 1971), pp. 227-278. For James as well as Henri Bergson, whom James quotes approvingly, sensible reality is too concrete to be entirely manageable. When we conceptualize, we cut out and fix some portion of the flux of sensible reality. Our concepts are an important step removed from reality and may be formulated in a clear and distinct fashion. But they do not match reality itself with precision.

[22]MR, pp. 70-72. The following example does not appear in Niebuhr's text. However, I believe that it expresses the sense of his epistemological discussion.

[23]"Life Is Worth Living," p. 4.

[24]Compare Niebuhr's refusal to equate knowledge with the mutual agreement or opinion of a community with Charles Pierce's reflections about the convergence of opinion within a community and the independence of reality from the thought of any individual or finite collection of individuals. Pierce also maintains what John E. Smith calls a realistic dimension. Changes of opinion come about by the experience of events beyond human control. See John E. Smith, Purpose and Thought: The Meaning of Pragmatism (New Haven: Yale University Press, 1978), pp. 17-18, 29-30.

[25]MR, p. 32.

[26]Ibid., p. 35.

[27]Ibid., p. 32.

[28]Brevard S. Childs, Biblical Theology in Crisis (Philadelphia: Westminster Press, 1970), pp. 16, 33-34.

[29]MR, p. 33.

[30]Ibid., p. 36.

[31]Ibid., p. 37.

[32]For example, Jews may regard themselves as heirs of the Exodus and Mosaic covenant. Christians may think of themselves as living between the time of Christ's incarnation and his return.

[33]MR, pp. 44-54.

[34]Ibid., pp. 44-45.

[35]Harvey, The Historian and the Believer, p. 252.

[36]Gordon D. Kaufman, Systematic Theology: A Historicist Perspective (New York: Charles Scribner's Sons, 1968), p. 26.

[37]MR, pp. 44-46.

[38]Ibid., p. 13.

[39]Ibid., p. 5.

[40]Ibid., p. 13.

[41]"Value Theory and Theology," pp. 93-106.

[42]KGA, pp. 12-15.

[43]MR, pp. 30-31.

[44]Ibid.

[45]Ibid., pp. 34-35.

[46]Julian N. Hartt, The Restless Quest (Philadelphia: United Church Press, A Pilgrim Press Book, 1975), p. 90.

[47]MR, p. 69.

[48]Ibid., p. 63.

[49]Ibid., p. 69.

[50]Ibid., pp. 91-93; H. Richard Niebuhr, "War As Crucifixion," The Christian Century 60 (April 1943): 513.

[51]MR, pp. 97-100.

[52]Ibid., pp. 74-75.

[53]Ibid., p. 80. See also Niebuhr's description of how American Protestants construct a unified vision of their experience with the aid of religious symbols in The Kingdom of God in America and chapter two of this dissertation.

[54]Ibid., p. 81.

[55]Ibid.

[56]Ibid., p. 82.

[57]Ibid., pp. 83-84.

[58]Ibid., p. 84.

[59]Ibid., p. 91.

[60]"War As Crucifixion," pp. 513-515.

[61]Ibid., p. 513.

[62]Ibid., p. 514.

[63]Ibid.

[64]H. Richard Niebuhr, "Is God in the War?" The Christian Century 59 (August 1942): 953-955.

[65]"War As Crucifixion," p. 515.

[66]Ibid., p. 514.

[67]Ibid., p. 515.

[68]H. Richard Niebuhr, "War as the Judgment of God," The Christian Century 59 (May 1942): 630-633.

[69]"Is God in the War?" p. 954.

[70]Ibid.

[71]MR, p. 92.

[72]"War as the Judgment of God," p. 931.

[73]Ibid., p. 95.

[74]Ibid., pp. 134, 137.

[75]Ibid., pp. 44-45; Harvey, The Historian and the Believer, pp. 234-242.

[76]There is nothing peculiar to theology in this; the same thing happens in other fields of inquiry and discourse. The Declaration of Independence says all men are created equal. But objections to this doctrine on the basis of biological inequalities miss the point. The dogma of equality is a moral claim which expresses faith in some value(s). Though biological principles of judgment may be relevant for some moral claims, priority is given to other principles of judgment in moral discourse. See William A. Christian, Oppositions of Religious Doctrines: A Study in the Logic of Dialogue Among Religions (New York: Herder and Herder, 1972), pp. 12-13; RM, pp. 74-75.

CHAPTER V

CHRIST AND CULTURE

Christ and Culture is a classic of theological
literature. As is well known, Niebuhr's typology furnishes a map of major alternatives in moral theology.
But it is equally important to observe that he constructs the types in accordance with a specific understanding of the content of theology, and that the typology as a whole clarifies his own transformationist
resolution of this content by comparing it with other
normative proposals.

For Niebuhr, the enduring debate about Christianity and civilization indicates the true dimensions
of the theological task. The debate began when Jesus,
himself a product of Jewish culture, confronted his
society with a hard challenge. It persists, for "not
only Jews but also Greeks and Romans, medievalists and
moderns, Westerners and Orientals have rejected Christ
because they saw in him a threat to their culture."[1]
Edward Gibbon, Karl Marx and others bring this tension
into the open and, says Niebuhr, their criticisms are
accurate to the extent that they point to a divergence
between the monotheism of Christian faith and the many
loyalties of culture.[2]

The tension between Christ and culture is primarily an internal problem for believers rather than an
ancillary difficulty for apologists.[3] The values and
accomplishments of the cultures in which believers reside as well as the Christ of the New Testament are in
the history Christians live and remember. Believers
are citizens of the city of man as well as the city of
God, and this dual citizenship makes the relation between Christ and culture a central feature of their
self-understandings. The recurrent issue of Christian
life is how the believer can be a loyal subject of
God's kingdom in the world. The classical problem of
Christian theology, then, is how loyalty to Christ relates to our diverse cultural loyalties.

Church history testifies that there is no
single answer to this problem, but only a series of
typical answers which represent phases of the church's
strategy in the world.[4] Each typical answer specifies
the content of "Christ" and "culture" in a different
way.[5] Nevertheless, there is sufficient unity in what
is meant by believers when they refer to Jesus Christ

and by people when they refer to culture to justify general definitions.[6]

Believing conceptions of Christ are related to "a definite character and person whose teachings, actions, and sufferings are of one piece."[7] As in The Meaning of Revelation, Niebuhr insists that the portrait of Christ in the New Testament remains the chief criterion and touchstone for theological notions about him.[8] There is a sense in which theological categories and propositions about Christ produce but partial translations of the original, first-order portraits.[9]

The inadequacy of many modern theologies stems from their unwillingness or inability to take the first-order portraits seriously. Liberals magnify Jesus' love, eschatologists his hope for the kingdom, and existentialists his obedience to God's command. Others exalt Jesus' humility. But each of these interpretations neglects the fact that Jesus practices all of these virtues. While a specific virtue may be selected for emphasis, each excellency leads to Jesus' irreducible relation to God.[10]

For Niebuhr, the meaning of Jesus Christ is best signified by the biblical symbol of sonship. This symbolic expression of Jesus' relation to God becomes the criterion for theological views of his person and authority. As son of God, Jesus points away from the many values and powers of historical and social existence toward the One who alone is good and powerful.[11] But Jesus Christ is not only the heroic example who points toward God. In his moral sonship, by his love, hope, obedience, faith, and humility in the presence of God, he is also the mediator of the Father's will toward humanity.[12]

Sonship to God the Father involves a "double movement--with men toward God, with God toward men; from the world to the Other, from the Other to the world."[13] This double movement, discernible in Jesus Christ himself, and not just in an external conflict between Christianity and civilization, is the true crux of the perennial problem of Christian faith. It is also the principal religious and theological warrant for attending to the claims of culture.

Niebuhr's preliminary definition of culture is non-theological, since each typical Christian answer specifies a particular theological interpretation. It is inclusive, since it needs to be applicable to the

diverse cultures in which believers reside. It strives
to take account of "that total process of human activity and that total result of such activity" which is
referred to by terms like "culture" and "civilization"
in ordinary speech.[14] Citing the anthropologist
Bronislaw Malinowski, Niebuhr claims that culture is

> the 'artificial, secondary environment' which
> man superimposes on the natural. It comprises
> language, habits, ideas, beliefs, customs,
> social organizations, inherited artifacts,
> technical processes and values.[15]

So conceived, culture reflects human purposiveness. Its achievements cannot be understood apart from
the ends or goals in the minds of its designers and
users. It is the sphere of human achievement concerned
with the realization of values.[16] The ends with which
cultural achievements are chiefly concerned are those
which contribute to the good for man. God or the gods
are held in high esteem because they advance human
self-realization.[17]

If Christ directs the believer toward the
transcendent God and then back again toward the world,
culture directs him toward a socially defined good for
man. Caught at the intersection of the dual movement
in Christ, believers are confronted with a vexing
difficulty.

> It is not essentially the problem of Christian-
> ity and civilization; for Christianity, whether
> defined as church, creed, ethics, or movement
> of thought, itself moves between the poles of
> Christ and culture. The relation of these
> two authorities constitutes its problem. When
> Christianity deals with the question of reason
> and revelation, what is ultimately in question
> is the relation of the revelation in Christ to
> the reason which prevails in culture. When it
> makes the effort to distinguish, contrast or
> combine rational ethics with its knowledge of
> the will of God, it deals with the understand-
> ing of right and wrong developed in the culture
> and with good and evil as illuminated by Christ
> . . . When the problem of loyalty to church or
> to state is raised, Christ and cultural society
> stand in the background as the true objects of
> devotion.[18]

This, then, is the main problem of Christian

theology. What is the appropriate relation between
faith in God through Christ and loyalty to culture?

The Logic of the Typical Answers

Niebuhr distinguishes five ways that Christians
have answered this question. Two may be characterized
as radical or extreme; the other three are closely related and belong "to that median type in which both
Christ and culture are distinguished and affirmed."[19]
He outlines four of the types with reference to scripture, a classical figure, and a nineteenth century
figure. This procedure supports the claim that the
answers recur and are not simply isolated products of
unrepeatable circumstances.

For example, those who insist that the two
authorities are opposed find scriptural support in
I John. In pre-modern times this stance is represented
by Tertullian and some monastic movements. Leo Tolstoy
articulates substantially the same answer in the nineteenth century, while Mennonites and other sectarians
traditionally view the relation between Christ and
culture in this way.

Though Niebuhr does not state it in an explicit
or mechanical fashion, he examines the inner logic of
each type with reference to the content of four polar
relations. Each typical answer is characterized by notions of Christ and culture that are informed by relations between reason and revelation, sin or evil and
good, law and gospel, and nature and grace.[20] These
polarities may be formulated as basic substantive
issues for theology and theological ethics. The relation between reason and revelation defines an epistemological issue. How do other types of knowledge relate
to revealed knowledge? The relation between sin or
evil and goodness raises the question of theodicy. Law
and gospel define the question of the ethical demand or
"oughtness" for theological ethics: How does faith and
knowledge of God affect conduct? Nature and grace
frame the question of the relation between God the
Creator and God the Redeemer, or the question of the
Trinity.[21]

Like the relation between Christ and culture,
each of these less inclusive themes may be resolved in
five typical ways. Thus, anticultural radicals like
Tertullian and Tolstoy tend to resolve the epistemological question so that revealed knowledge is resolutely
separate from and at odds with what is known through

cultural reason. They view grace and the world as
culture as two opposing forces.

Though Niebuhr does not address the question of
theological discourse in Christ and Culture, each typical answer also tends to approach and resolve this issue
in a distinct way. Thus, for "against culture" Christians, theological discourse is highly confessional and
closely tied to the religious language of the believing
community. Theology is entirely separate from cultural
forms of discourse, whether the latter be ordinary,
philosophical, aesthetic, or scientific. A theology of
this type generally does not claim to be communicative
currency beyond the confines of the Christian community.
The case is quite different, however, among theologians
who see a fundamental agreement between Christ and
culture, reason and revelation, and so on.

The actual emergence of theological positions
and ways of Christian life is complex. For Niebuhr,
Christians are profoundly shaped by their experience,
which includes some exposure to the tradition of the
historic communities in which they participate. There
is no reason to assume that they work inductively from
resolutions of the basic polarities toward definitions
of Christ and culture or deductively from definitions
of Christ and culture toward statements of the less inclusive relations.[22] Possibly, an impression of Jesus
Christ mediated by a believing community will dominantly influence a definition of the less inclusive relations. However, it is just as possible that a forceful
apprehension of sin, or some combination of apprehensions will dominantly influence a theological stance
and way of Christian living. The two are inevitably
intertwined.

If the actual emergence of a theological stance
is more complex than the types indicate, it is also the
case that no person or group conforms completely to a
type.[23] Important individuals and movements exhibit
characteristics of more than one of the types.[24] As
heuristic instruments, the types allow us to plot the
great motifs that recur "in the long wrestling of
Christians with their enduring problem." They are not
exact copies of reality, but imaginative constructs
that are by no means wholly exclusive.[25]

The Typical Christian Answers

Niebuhr begins his analysis with the two
extreme positions. "Against culture" Christians

99

uncompromisingly affirm Christ's sole authority and reject culture's claims.[26] Like the writer of I John,
they focus attention on the lordship of Christ.[27] They
also tend to emphasize Christ as the giver of a new law
and commandment. During the second century, anticultural Christians interpret Jesus as the founder and king
of a new society, or people. Tertullian views the son
of God as the great authoritative teacher,[28] while Leo
Tolstoy regards Christ's commandments as "a statement
of God's eternal law" that abrogates the law of Moses.[29]

The attempt to build a holy society exclusively
around Jesus leads to a sharp condemnation of culture.
Tertullian understands the fall as a catastrophe which
divides created nature from corrupted culture, and
counsels believers to withdraw from the corrupted
entertainments, learning, offices, and occupations of
civilization. For Tolstoy, church, state, and private
property are devilish citadels of evil. He counsels
intellectuals, landlords, and artists to engage in man-
ual labor. He insists that the sciences are vain, and
that the only good art is one which provides a sincere
communication of feeling, is comprehensible to the
masses, and accords with Christian morality.[30]

Without representatives of the radical answer,
says Niebuhr, other Christian groups tend to lose their
balance and reduce Christian faith to a utilitarian
device.[31] In this respect, radical Christianity is a
necessary phase of the strategy of the church in the
world. But the radical alternative is inadequate "because it affirms in words what it denies in action;
namely, the possibility of sole dependence on Jesus
Christ to the exclusion of culture."[32]

This objection stems from Niebuhr's conviction that the reality of God is mediated through social
and historical experience. No one comes to Christ as
an acultural being: "Christ claims no man purely as a
natural being, but always as one who has become human
in a culture."[33] The radical who separates reason and
revelation is finally unable to formulate a rule of
Christian life and practice without using elements of
cultural reasoning. Though Athens may have little to
do with Jerusalem, Tertullian cannot describe the Trinity without recourse to the vocabulary of Latin jurists.
Like Tolstoy, he is driven to an artificial distinction
between "natural" knowledge, the reason of the uncor-
rupted human soul which is an acceptable instrument
of Christian life and theology, and vitiated cultural
understanding.[34]

This distinction implies a restriction of sin and evil to culture. By contrast, the holy community called out from the world and exempted from infirmities becomes the pure locus of grace and goodness. Radical Christians are therefore unable to frame a truly universal doctrine of sin. They also come perilously close to the notion that the creative and providential activity of God is entirely separate from his localized redemption in Jesus Christ. When the activity of the triune God breaks the artificial distinction between nature and culture, nature and grace, like reason and revelation, end in resolute opposition. The common grace of God the creator and sustainer which upholds nature and history becomes divorced from his saving grace.

By contrast, Christians who recognize a fundamental agreement between Christ and culture interpret Christ as the messiah of their society, the fulfiller of its best hopes, and the perfector of its true faith.[35] "Christ is identified with what men conceive to be their finest ideals, their noblest institutions, and their best philosophy."[36] Ebionites, for example, identify the revealed messiah with the expected one, and interpret Jesus as the fulfillment of their Jewish cultural tradition.[37] Gnostics accommodate Christ to Hellenistic wisdom, and view him as the great revealer of the truth that sets people free from the prison of flesh and the world.[38]

In the modern period, the "of culture" alternative is expressed by enlightened representatives of eighteenth century reason who seek and find an eminently reasonable Christ. Thomas Jefferson looks upon Christ as the perfect moral educator and excises from the gospels those sayings which the educator would not have uttered. Immanuel Kant writes of a Christianity within the limits of pure reason.[39] Albrecht Ritschl, a nineteenth century architect of this position, transmutes the religion of reason into the religion of humanity.[40] Despite his allegiance to a confessional method, Ritschl takes the will of man to master nature as well as the New Testament as his dual starting point,[41] and his theology virtually reverses the anticultural alternative.

Again, nature and culture are artificially distinguished. For Ritschl, however, the true conflict is between man and nature rather than the believer and culture. God's kingdom is the ultimate triumph of spirit over nature. Divine activity becomes genuine

101

culture's greatest ally in the business of realizing the perfect ethical and spiritual commonwealth.

Like the anticultural radicals, cultural Christians distinguish reason and revelation as different sources of insight. Unlike the radicals, however, they tend to view reason as the final arbiter of truth. Revelation becomes the presentation to less able minds of rational truth clad in mythical garments. It is the religious name for the growth of reason in history.

The best cultural reasoning confirms revelation.[42] The moral teaching of Jesus agrees with the highest ethical wisdom of western culture. And, for many nineteenth century liberals, this essential correspondence is a basis for demonstrating Christianity's absoluteness and superiority among the world's religions.

Anticultural radicals find it difficult to accept orthodox trinitarian theology because they can accept no substantial continuity between redemptive grace in Christ and the processes of history. Cultural Christians have the same problem for the opposite reason. Identifying Jesus with the immanent divine spirit at work in people and in history, they find it difficult to distinguish God's redemptive grace in Christ from the providential divine governance of the world. Their effort to interpret Jesus as the Christ of culture ends in the inability to distinguish the immanent development of human culture from the redemptive, eschatological work of divine grace.

These difficulties relate to the rise of a new and subtle legalism.[43] The emphasis on human effort to build God's kingdom on earth or to effect the soul's release from this world, does not lead to the biblicist legalism typical of the against culture group. Instead, it sanctions a self-reliant humanism which pursues the common good and goal of humanity. In an attempt to hold human effort and divine activity together, for example, Ritschl identifies faithfulness in one's social and civil calling as a prerequisite for God's kingdom.

The attempt to hold divine activity and human effort together in this fashion also leads cultural Christians to posit a realm free from the disabling influences of sin.[44] If radicals find the holy community free from disease, liberals posit purity in the moment of _gnosis_ or in the good will which enables human effort to hit its ultimate mark. The believer who understands how his social calling contributes to God's kingdom and the revolutionary who participates in the enlightening experience of social oppression are thought to be better suited to comprehend the true meaning of the gospel and to join the struggle.

The radical's resolution of the basic polarities expresses the belief that God reveals himself exclusively in the life and teachings of Jesus Christ, and that when one follows Christ, one rejects the claims of culture. By contrast, the liberal's resolution supports the belief that God is acting to overcome nature and to bring culture to fulfillment. This divergence is reflected also in their views of integrity and intelligibility. For "against culture" Christians, integrity means adequacy to a deposit of revealed knowledge of God separate from the accumulated wisdom of culture. Intelligibility means adequacy to the believer's experience of division from meanings and values in the wider society. Just as the radical tends to view the Christian life as single-minded reliance on the law of Christ purged of all cultural values, he also tends to think that faith seeking understanding pursues a single-minded exposition of revelation purged of all cultural reasoning. An adequate presentation of Christian doctrine consists essentially in a formally ordered, exclusively revelational content. Usually, the content of revelation (and so also of doctrine) is thought to be purely biblical.

Proponents of this type of theology tend to understand religious language as speech about God and man based exclusively in special revelation. Theology is the disciplined, orderly presentation of this religious speech. There is a tendency to understand theological discourse as the rightly ordered exposition of the distinct speech of the religious community about God and humanity. Ideally, both the religious idiom of the community and its theological language remain resolutely separate from all philosophies and cultural forms of discourse.

It is hardly surprising that anticultural Christians often display an antipathy toward comprehensive theological statements. They are suspicious of systematic theology, and sometimes of all theology, because they believe that the introduction of a logical scheme of order or presentation threatens the entrance of foreign cultural elements into talk about God. When and if references to cultural practices, ideas, and

philosophies appear in radical theologies, they usually
serve to clarify Christian practice and doctrine by way
of contrast.

However, even writers who wish to frame a theology that nowhere transgresses the bounds of strictly
confessional discourse sometimes attempt comprehensive
dogmatic statements. According to Karl Barth, for example, Jesus Christ is the sole criterion of theology.
Dogmatics is theologia crucis, an act of obedience to
Jesus Christ.[45] It is a strictly confessional enterprise that reflects on the religious speech of the
church and guards faith from dangerous cultural
impurities.[46]

What Niebuhr says about radical attempts to
order Christian life may also be said of attempts to
order theology in sole dependence upon biblical revelation and the religious language of the community. They
tend to affirm in programmatical declarations what they
deny in execution. When Barth considers moral issues,
like relations between men and women and the respect
due human life, he discusses apparently natural orders
in relations among persons, distinguishes subordination
from inequality, and affirms that human life by its
very nature consists in solidarity with others.[47]

If the tendency of anticultural theologians is
to appeal to the word of God as the sole criterion for
the adequacy of theological statements, cultural Christians tend to judge the adequacy of theology in light
of cultural reason. The characteristic appeals and
warrants for theological statements differ widely between the two camps. For cultural Christians, integrity means adequacy to a revelation which fulfills and
perfects the best wisdom of culture. Intelligibility
means adequacy to the believer's sense that Christ
fulfills his cultural cause, and expresses the essential harmony between revelation and reason. An adequate theological statement, then, accords with what
can be known through cultural reasoning.

Liberal Christians tend to understand religious
speech as the language of the Christian community about
God and humanity which enables a demonstrably true interpretation of the human situation. To specify this
interpretation, they often think it necessary to separate the kernel of meaning in religious discourse from
its stylistic and conceptual peculiarities. Theology
becomes the disciplined development and presentation of
the basic meaning of religious language about the human

104

situation in terms of contemporary cultural insights and understanding. Ideally, it is doubly intelligible, persuasive to believers and unbelievers alike, because it presents the most adequate available interpretation of cultural experience.

Niebuhr's criticism of the Christ of culture stance can be extended to liberal notions of theological discourse. Cultural theologians tend to accomodate Christian insights to culture to the extent that it becomes difficult to distinguish theology from the development of cultural forms of discourse. One may legitimately ask whether Christian theology understood in this way has anything distinctive to say to the world, whether the good illuminated by Christ is really different from understandings of the good developed in culture and so on. Precisely because it claims to represent the essential self-understanding of culture, this type of theology seems to reduce itself to a philosophy, albeit the true one, among many others.

For Niebuhr, these extreme positions remain less than adequate expressions of the double movement in Christ. Radical Christianity tends to move away from culture toward God and so produce a theology within the limits of deity. On the other hand, cultural Christianity moves away from God toward culture and so gives rise to a theology within the limits of humanity.

These criticisms are not surprising. With reference to the epistemological question, the two extreme types correspond to the positions of crisis and liberal theologians. Again, Niebuhr is concerned to explore alternatives to these two dominant movements. By 1951, however, he is able to specify these alternatives in terms of the relation between Christ and culture. More adequate understandings of the problem of Christianity belong to a median type in which both Christ and culture are distinguished and affirmed.[48] Furthermore, he now recognizes three mediating or "centrist" alternatives.

The Church of the Center

Unlike anticultural radicals and accommodators of Christ to culture, the great majority movement in Christianity understands the fundamental issue to lie between God and man rather than Christ and the world.[49] This different view can be formulated in terms of the four theological polarities. For all three centrist groups, Jesus is primarily the son of God. A trinitarian emphasis requires that God's redemptive work and his creative, providential work be integrally related. Christ and the world, whether the latter be conceived primarily as nature or as culture, cannot be simply opposed since the world as nature is God's creation, and culture "cannot exist save as it is upheld by the creator and governor of nature."[50] Simplistic divisions between nature and culture become unacceptable.

According to Niebuhr, centrist Christians also agree that people are "in the realm of God by divine ordering under divine orders."[51] Obedience is to be rendered in the concrete natural and cultural affairs of human life. In this situation, centrists both distinguish and affirm human reason and effort and divine revelation and activity. Revelation and reason, grace and works are dialectically related. No concrete act of obedience to God is possible without the use of human intelligence and will.

Since centrists reject simple divisions between nature and culture, they are convinced that people cannot find a pure gnosis or will within themselves as individuals or communities called out from the world. Unlike gnostics and Ritschlian liberals, they believe that sin is radical. It infects the inner recesses of the human spirit. Unlike the radicals Tertullian and Tolstoy, they believe that sin is universal. There is no special community exempted from its effects.

Finally, centrist agreement about nature and grace, sin and evil, reason and revelation, is connected with a common conviction about grace and law. On the one hand, centrists maintain the priority of gospel forgiveness over human works precisely because sin is radical and universal. On the other, since they believe that culture is upheld by grace and that people are in the realm of God under divine orders, they recognize the necessity for lawful works of obedience. "They cannot separate the works of culture from the grace of God" since those works are enabled by grace. They cannot separate their experience of grace from cultural activity because love to the unseen God requires service in his visible kingdom.[52]

Within this general field of agreement, however, significantly different nuances are associated with different ways of Christian life and diverse understandings of theology. Representatives of the Christ above culture type find scriptural support in passages like Romans 13:16 ("The authorities are

106

ministers of God.") which imply a synthesis of Christ and culture. Thus, Clement of Alexandria tempers Christian behavior with the best cultural training and education.[53] Thomas Aquinas, prime representative of the synthetic group, tries to combine Christian faith with the "new knowledge" available in the writings of Aristotle.

The christological fulcrum of this stance is an understanding of distinction within basic unity. Christ is both God and man in one person. His two natures are neither confused nor separated.[54] Often, as for the Alexandrian theologians, Christ is regarded as both Logos and Lord.[55] As Logos, he is the reason or wisdom of God active in the order of creation and intimately involved in culture. At the same time, however, he stands above the world as its transcendent Lord and cannot be interpreted in simply cultural terms. Thus, if Clement is concerned to identify positive connections between the teachings of Jesus and cultural norms, he also realizes that Jesus' radical utterances go far beyond cultural expectations.[56] This same duality is reflected also in the synthesist's notion of culture. On the one hand, culture is the product of human freedom. On the other, it is upheld by God's grace and order. Culture is a realm to which divine action and revelation as well as human effort and reason apply.

For Niebuhr, the Thomistic synthesis is closely informed by "the conviction of which Trinitarian doctrine is a verbal expression: namely, that the Creator of nature and Jesus Christ and the immanent spirit are one essence."[57] Nature is ordered toward the good by God's creative and providential activity. Its order indicates God's purposes and requirements for humanity. Yet Thomas "does not try to disguise the gulf that lies between Christ and culture."[58] The happiness attainable through the work of culture upon and within creation is imperfect. Beyond it lies another, perfect and eternal end "for which all striving is an inadequate preparation."[59] Unlike cultural Christians, Thomas sharply distinguishes achievements of culture from the divinely appointed end of humanity.

This establishes the priority of grace in Thomas' system. People are able to know and to puruse natural good by the exercise of their natural endowments, though even here the help of God as first mover is necessary. Moreover, for people to know, do, and wish their supernatural end, God must gracefully add

certain principles and qualities to human nature. On
the basis of these superadded elements, people co-
operate with divine grace to merit what would otherwise be impossible: namely, eternal life.[60]

   The themes of duality and cooperation are also
present in Thomas' theory of law.[61] By reasoning on
the basis of natural law, people devise positive rules
to guide human life. These rules have their source in
the objective natural order which itself is ultimately
based on the law in the eternal reason of God.[62] But
Thomas also insists on the necessity of revealed law
in addition to the human law derived from nature.[63]
Found in scripture and especially in Christ, divine
law is partly coincident with positive law and partly
transcends it. Revealed law is necessary to direct
human actions toward the supernatural end which transcends man's natural faculties.[64] As Niebuhr explains
it,

> "Thou shalt not steal" is a command found both
> by reason and in revelation; "Sell all that
> thou hast and give it to the poor" is found
> in the divine law only. It applies to man as
> one who has a virtue implanted in him beyond
> the virtue of honesty, and who has been
> directed in hope toward a perfection beyond
> justice in this mortal existence.[65]

Thomas' theory of law reflects his view of the relation
between reason and revelation. Faith and knowledge
proceed from the same divine source.[66] God not only
reveals certain truths to people; he also guides
reasoning along a straight path and removes ignorance
from speculative and practical judgments about created
things by the gift of knowledge.[67] Some revealed
truths, like the existence of God and the immortality
of the soul, are also known by reason alone. Because
they are attainable by natural reason, they are considered necessary presuppositions for faith. By re-
vealing these truths, God enables all people to grasp
saving knowledge with certitude, and without engaging
in the rigors of metaphysical speculation.

   A second group of revealed truths contains the
proper articles of faith which surpass the faculties of
the human mind. Doctrines of the Trinity, the Incarnation, and redemption belong to this class. These must
be believed since reason can neither demonstrate them
to be true nor prove them to be false.[68]

For Niebuhr, the synthesist expresses an important principle which no other group seems to express
so well: "namely, the principle that the Creator and
the Savior are one, or that whatever salvation means
beyond creation it does not mean destruction of the
created."[69] Writers like Clement and Thomas affirm
that the conduct of Christians cannot fall short of
the standards of cultural achievement, however high
they may rise above them. They recognize an important
area where the concerns of believers and nonbelievers
coincide.

But precisely this area of cooperation and co-
incidence between grace and culture, revelation and
reason raises a critical point. The effort to join
Christ and culture, God's work and man's, the eternal
and the temporal into a single system seems to absolutize what is relative. The genuine order of nature
which indicates God's purposes and requirments for
humanity may be too easily identified with particular
interpretations of that order by a culturally conditioned reason.[70] Standards of human conduct determined
by a conditioned reason may then be elevated to the
rank of the purposes and requirements of God. In this
sense, the synthesist may be criticized for a lack of
historical understanding.[71]

For Niebuhr, this is exactly what takes place
in the discourses of Pope Leo XIII. Though Leo called
for a new synthesis of Christ and culture, he actually
supported the re-establishment of a synthesis with the
culture, reason, and morality of the middle ages. In
this respect, the thought of Leo and many nineteenth
century Thomists mirrors the pattern of cultural
Protestantism. For Leo, as for Albrecht Ritschl,
Christ is interpreted through culture, though the
culture is that of the thirteenth rather than the
nineteenth century.

Behind this objection stands a more specific
criticism. The synthesist seems to have a less than
radical doctrine of sin, one which exempts human reason
from some of sin's effects. Believers more prone to
notice the many instances that reasoned argument has
been used in the service of self-interest and the
status quo find a certain naïvete in the claim that
God aids and directs human reasoning along the straight
path of justice.[72]

This resolution of the basic polarities leads
to the belief that God is acting to fulfill the best

features of culture in a way that goes beyond our cultural expectations. For the synthesist, integrity
means adequacy to a revelation which goes beyond the
accumulated wisdom of culture, but nevertheless, completes it. Intelligibility means adequacy to the believer's sense of the fulfillment of culture that culture itself does not provide. Unlike radical Christians, the synthesist characteristically appeals both
to cultural reasoning and to revelation as criteria for
theological statements. Unlike the cultural Christian,
however, he does not simply equate the two. Some theological statements express complete agreement between
cultural wisdom and revelation. Others go beyond the
best cultural reason, though they are in essential harmony with its dominant direction. Adequate doctrines
exemplify the synthesis.

For "above culture" Christians, reasoned interpretations of the human situation point beyond themselves and are in need of fulfillment. Religious language goes beyond reasoned interpretations, enabling a
more complete interpretation of humanity and its ultimate context. Thus, for Thomas, reason demonstrates
that God exists as first cause and mover. Revelation
is in harmony with these statements and, indeed, presupposes them. But it goes beyond them to explain
the character of God's will for humanity, his love,
justice, and mercy as well as the appropriateness of
the incarnation.[73]

It is not surprising that Christians interested
in a synthesis of grace and nature, God's work and
man's, the eternal and the temporal, often favor systematic theological statements. It would seem to follow logically, perhaps even psychologically, that synthesists are suspicious of any statement, whether philosophical or religious, that cannot be displayed in its
comprehensive relations to other truths found by reason
or in revelation. Since other Christians often criticize this systematic tendency, it is important to
recognize the deeply religious conviction that supports it. The synthesist's fundamental belief is that
the Creator of nature, the Redeemer, and the immanent
Spirit are one essence. Though this trinitarian emphasis may imply a system of three truths,[74] it def-
initely requires that all truth spring from a single
divine source.

Again, Niebuhr's basic criticism may be extended to synthetic notions of theological discourse.
Synthesists tend to join Christian insights and cul-

tural reasoning to the point where faith is tied to the insights of a particular culture. A particular philosophy is often elevated to the rank of an indispensible presupposition for intelligent faith. Perhaps a synthetic answer is possible in which it is recognized that the reasoning which aids theological construction is as much a part of the temporal order as are other human achievements. But it is hard to see how a synthesis of faith and reason can be recognized as provisional, subject to radical attack, transformation, and replacement without losing its character as a genuine synthesis.[75]

Strong criticisms of attempts to synthesize Christ and culture have come from dualist Christians. Like all centrists, dualists hold together loyalty to Christ and responsibility to culture. Unlike synthesists, however, they believe that people are involved in an overt rebellion against God's rule. Conflict between the righteousness of God and the righteousness of self becomes the fundamental issue of religious life.[76] Since the relation of these principles is paradoxical, there is no possibility for synthesis or cooperation.

Advocates of this stance find scriptural support in the tension between human righteousness and the goodness of God in the Pauline epistles.[77] Martin Luther, the chief representative of the dualist pattern, upholds the same tension by sharply distinguishing law from gospel, and the earthly from the heavenly kingdom.[78] In the nineteenth century a dualism of the infinite and the finite characterizes the writings of Søren Kierkegaard.[79]

The dualist's fundamental belief is that God freely forgives people without any merit on their part.[80] Christ is the mediator who reconciles God and humanity, the agent of divine grace and forgiveness who remains faithful despite rebellion against him.[81] By contrast, culture is the realm of human works. Human achievements are expressions of godlessness or the will to be secure and to live without being indebted to or forgiven by God.[82] The disease of sin infects all cultural conventions and institutions. It is manifest even in the piety of those who fancy themselves possessors of divine righteousness.

The dualist differs from the synthesist in his understanding of the extent and thoroughness of human depravity.[83] Whereas Aquinas believes that revealed

111

truths are compatible with the best human reasoning,
Luther regards human reasoning as darkness before the
holiness of God. Reason cannot be joined in harmony
with God's revealed truth, since it is exercised in
the service of radically sinful dispositions to self-
sufficiency and independence.

"Hence the dualist joins the radical Christian
in pronouncing the whole world of human culture to be
godless and sick unto death."[84] But he differs from
the radical in his understanding of the universality of
sin and divine providence. The dualist knows that he
belongs to culture and cannot get out of it. He does
not exempt the Christian community from the effects of
sin. At the same time, he believes that people are
sustained in culture by the activity of God. Unlike
the radical who virtually separates God from culture,
the dualist is convinced that even this sinful world
cannot exist apart from divine providence.

In this situation the dualist's conduct as well
as his language tends to become paradoxical.[85] The
believer is a sinner, yet righteous. He lives under
the law, but also under grace. He knows God in whom he
trusts, yet walks by faith, not sight. He stands on
the side of sinful humanity, yet seeks to interpret the
word of God in an earthly tongue.

These tensions and dualities are visible in the
theology of Martin Luther. For Luther the demand of
the gospel is the absolute requirement of an absolute
God.[86] Sin, understood as a fundamental disposition of
the heart or spring of human actions, makes it impossible for people to fulfill this demand. "Experience
bears witness that whatever good we perform, this
tendency toward evil remains, and no one is ever
cleansed of it." [87]

As lawgiver, Christ convicts people of their
sinfulness. "He shows them that an evil tree cannot
bring forth good fruits,"[88] that good works cannot
make a person good, and that self-sufficiency is a
counsel of despair. Humanity is caught between good
and evil, salvation and utter estrangement. The sole
source of hope is that God reckons people righteous
apart from their works, and does not count their sins
against them. In those led to despair of their own
merit, miraculous and free justification leads to a
change of heart and love of neighbor.

Nevertheless, the fact that Christians begin

anew with the revelation of God's grace does not change the basic duality of sin and grace.[89] Christians are counted righteous more than they are made righteous. They are righteous by proxy rather than infusion. Grace is not joined to the soul as a new quality or virtue. It is never embodied as a capacity exercised with regularity in concert with human wills. For Luther, "the saints are always sinners."[90] Even after the gift of justification this is "not a life of sinlessness with the cure completed" but a life of tension and struggle. The Christian is sick and well at the same time; "the church is the inn and the infirmary for those who are sick and in need of being made well."[91]

This duality is reflected by the believer's residence in two kingdoms, the one spiritual and ordered toward eternity, the other temporal and passing away. As one turned toward God, the believer's heart and inner disposition participate in the freedom of the heavenly kingdom. God is merciful, governing with his right hand through gospel to bring people to eternal life. As a participant in the external orders and occupations of this rebellious world, however, the believer remains subject to the earthly kingdom where God judges and restrains chaotic evil through civil laws and magistrates. "A Christian is a perfectly free lord of all, subject to none," but also "a perfectly dutiful servant of all, subject to all."[92] Both realms are ruled by the one God though they are governed to different purposes.

Christ converts the springs of human action. His forgiveness provides a dispositional freedom in moral life and establishes a community of spiritual reconciliation within which the struggles of the heart take place. But he does not directly govern external actions or construct a new temporal society in which people carry on their work.[93]

The same duality is visible in Luther's estimate of reason.[94] Not only are laws requiring specific works necessary to govern affairs in the earthly kingdom, but reason and philosophy also have their legitimate place in the temporal order. Reason is instrumental for building sound houses and founding governments. It is the soul of laws that restrain social anarchy and maintain civil order. But it is blind in holy affairs where people must do what is acceptable to God. Bound to the juridical logic of merit and self-sufficiency, reason, like law, can only regard God's free justification as incomprehensible folly. It therefore passes beyond its competency when it wanders into the heavenly kingdom and meddles with matters of faith that are governed by the revelation of God's grace.[95]

For Niebuhr, this dualistic pattern presents a profound report of Christian experience.[96] "Far more than any of the preceding groups," dualists "take into account the dynamic character of God, man, grace and sin."[97] The emphasis on experience and dynamism leads to a model for morality that focuses more on styles of life than on specific and sometimes contrived lists of prescribed deeds and virtues. But sharp distinctions between the works of men and God's grace, between the laws of society and divine forgiveness, and between the voices of reason and gospel revelation, leave room for criticisms of the dualistic pattern.

The dualist has a tendency virtually to join temporality and finitude to sin, to virtually collapse creation and fall into a single event. In the writings of Paul, creation is used primarily to reinforce the condemnation of all men because of sin.[98] For Luther, who sometimes refers to sin as a "defect" of human nature,[99] there is a sense in which the wrath of God is directed not only against sin, but against the whole temporal world. This tendency raises the question of whether the dualist pattern undesirably demeans the temporal order, and does less than justice to the creative and providential activity of God.[100]

Given this theological context, it is difficult to avoid the conclusion that the dualist tends to place far greater emphasis on response to the gospel and divine forgiveness than on obedience to the standards of a dying culture. Certainly, says Niebuhr, a Paul or a Luther does not intend to make obedience to the laws of culture a matter of indifference. Yet whether or not this is their intention, a tendency toward antinomianism sometimes results.[101]

When the dualist's distinction between the law and gospel is combined with a sharp distinction between temporal and eternal kingdoms, it becomes difficult to see how gospel is present in temporal affairs. The dualist both desires and requires improvements in the conduct of princes, citizens, tradesmen, and slaves. But these improvements take place within an essentially unchanged social context.[102]

Conservatism is a logical consequence of the

114

tendency to think of law, state, and other institutions as restraining forces, dykes against sin, preventers of anarchy, rather than as positive agencies through which men in social union render positive service to neighbors advancing toward true life.[103]

This resolution of the substantive polarities leads to the belief that God is overcoming evil with his right hand by freely forgiving sin and with his left hand by preserving culture as a dyke against chaos. Integrity means adequacy to a revelation in paradox with cultural wisdom. Intelligibility means adequacy to the believer's sense of duality between faith in Christ and the values of culture. Theology is primarily the proclamation of the gospel of free justification, and the chronicle of spiritual struggle between the righteousness of God and human self-centeredness.[104]

The unreasonable fact of divine forgiveness drives a wedge between theology and other forms of discourse. Theology offers the true interpretation of our spiritual life in relation to God.[105] Insofar as reasoned accounts appear in theologies of this type, they tend to function as accounts of man's cultural life which have little to do with accounts of his spirituality from the vantage point of divine forgiveness. So, for example, reasoned discourses about merit and civil justice are sharply contrasted with forgiveness through grace; philosophical and cultural notions of love are sharply distinguished from agape.

In some respects, the dualist's view of religious and theological discourse is similar to the view of the Christian radical. But the dualist differs from the radical in that he recognizes a legitimate place for the exercise of human reason. He therefore finds himself obligated not only to purge theology of cultural impurities, but also to keep theological terms and insights from being misapplied to worldly affairs. Thus, Luther finds it necessary to criticize those who would apply the spiritual freedom of the gospel directly to social concerns as well as to remove philosophical speculation from matters of faith. The dualist recognizes the legitimacy of a distinct Christian theology and the legitimacy of distinct forms of cultural discourse. He is, therefore, often called upon to set the boundaries within which each reigns supreme.

An adequate presentation of doctrine tends to distinguish a specific territory of experience and meaning for theological statements. Adequacy to the lived experience of grace remains the primary criterion, but the experience of grace is not to be confused with other human experiences. This leads some dualists to attempt comprehensive expositions of Christian doctrine in its multifaceted relations to other forms of discourse. But these expositions are not synthetic. Their principal objective is to distinguish theology from cultural forms of discourse.

As with the other types, however, Niebuhr's criticisms of this pattern may also be extended to its notions of theological discourse. Dualists tend to distinguish Christian insights from those of the surrounding culture to the point where faith and theology become compartmentalized. In the area of morality, for example, Christian faith and theology seem never truly to confront the claims of reasoned laws and concepts of justice. Despite their recognition of the cultural sphere, dualists characteristically separate the insights of faith from cultural ideas since the latter are but products of a sick and dying order. Theology tends to take both the challenge and the promise of cultural meanings and values less than seriously, and to leave them unchanged in a way that would be unacceptable were they regarded as created vessels that might be converted to the service of true life.

The conversionist's understanding of Christ and culture is closest to dualism but also has affinities with with other patterns. Like dualists, conversionists believe that culture is enmeshed in self-destructiveness and contradiction. At the same time, however, they believe that culture is under God's sovereign rule, entrusted to Christ's merciful and redeeming care. It is the divinely appointed arena for human faithfulness and obedience.

Representatives of this pattern tend to refer to Christ as Redeemer more than as Lawgiver. Certainly, Christ tries and judges human hearts, but he also heals their most virulent disease and enables new life. He is the ruler of human hearts, the fountain of human life and behavior, who holds forth the possibility of renewal through redemptive grace.

Conversionists find scriptural support in the powerful way the writer of the gospel of John joins creation and redemption through incarnation.106 The motif is visible in Augustine's view of history, and in John Calvin's appreciation for the positive

116

capabilities of cultural vocations and institutions to
promote divine purposes. It emerges also in John
Wesley's hope for a present transformation of men into
sons of God, and in Jonathan Edwards' understanding of
conversion. During the nineteenth century, says
Niebuhr, conversionism reaches its clearest expression
in the writings of F. D. Maurice.

     "What distinguishes conversionists from dual-
ists is their more positive and hopeful attitude toward
culture."[107] This different attitude is connected with
theological convictions about creation, the fall, and
history. The conversionist tends to interpret the
creative activity of "Christ-in-God" as a major theme.
This christological nuance is an attempt to state that
God's creative activity is closely connected with his
redemptive activity; that the theme of creation through
Christ is "neither overpowered by nor overpowering the
idea of atonement."[108] Connected with the agency of
redemption, creation becomes more than prologue to the
fall or an arena for the restraint of evil. It is the
kingdom of Christ under Christ's rule. Indeed, the
conversionist sharply distinguishes the fall from creation. Human nature is a created good that has been
corrupted through the misuse of freedom. The fall is
moral and personal rather than metaphysical. Whereas
the dualist regards the problem of culture as one of
how it may restrain evil, the conversionist looks for
the positive reorientation of culture toward the purposes of God.

     The conversionist's convictions about creation
and the fall are closely connected with a distinct view
of history. Radicals view history as the story of a
rising church and a dying culture; for the cultural
Christian, it is the story of the Spirit's encounter
with nature. Synthesists view history as the period of
preparation for an ultimate communion of the soul with
God; for the dualist, it is the time between the giving
of the promise and its fulfillment. For the conversionist, history is the dramatic interaction between
humanity and the God for whom all things are possible.
Divine activity enables a present renewal of historical
realities. Even a corrupted culture can become a
transformed life in and to the glory of God.[109]

     For the conversionist, nature and grace cannot
be separated or opposed since the very agency of redemption is involved in the order of creation. Calvin
believes that God's glory is proclaimed by the beauty
and symmetry of humanity, the order of creation, and

the governance of history. It is axiomatic that sin is not created human nature, but its derangement.[110] Redemptive grace regenerates, restores, and transforms created nature; it does not destroy or replace nature. Hence the conversionist joins the synthesist in pronouncing the world of creation good.

Like the dualist, however, the conversionist believes that humanity has entered upon a course of corruption and disorder which disturbs every phase of life. F. D. Maurice sees a denial of created goodness in a selfishness that insinuates itself even into the exclusivism and self-righteousness of religious people.[111] Sin is the principle of self-love, a rebellion against God and a refusal to acknowledge indebtedness to God in Christ.[112] It is a moral sickness that infects human justice and extends even to rational life, turning the wisdom of men into folly.

These convictions lead to a strong sense of the priority of grace over works. For Augustine as for Jonathan Edwards, humanity is caught in the denial of the law of its own being. As long as self-love remains the controlling orientation or affection of the self, it is not possible either to know or to will the good. A fundamental reorientation of the wellspring of human will and reason is needed to free human capacities from bondage. Transformation by grace is man's only hope. At the same time, convictions about the goodness of the created order and the possibility of divine renewal lead the conversionist to maintain that institutions, laws, and conventions need not function exclusively as dykes against sin, but may also be directed toward the true good. Grace transforms law so that it becomes an instrument for the positive ordering of life toward God.[113]

How conversion differs from the redirection of human faculties spoken of by the synthesist can be clarified with reference to the question of reason and revelation. As we have seen, Aquinas maintains that the best natural reasoning is able to grasp some revealed truths. Other revealed truths go beyond the best reasoning, but harmonize with it. When added to the truths knowable by reason, they complete the knowledge of divine things necessary for salvation. Revelation cooperates with reason, directs it to its own best products, and orients it toward the appropriate transcendent object.

For Augustine and Calvin, however, the residual

118

human awareness of a transcendent power is so corrupted by the disease of sin that natural knowledge about the gods remains skewed and confused, a mere shadow image of the truth. Chained to the service of self-love, reason fashions gods in its own image. True knowledge of divine things requires a change in the fundamental love or affection of the self. Once this affective basis for reason is converted, reasoning begins anew, oriented in a different direction. Faith does not supplement the best reasoning so much as it forms the basis for a reconstruction of our lines of reasoning. The life of reason

> . . . is reoriented and redirected by being
> given a new first principle. Instead of begin-
> ning with faith in itself and with love of its
> own order, the reasoning of redeemed man begins
> with faith in God and love of the order which
> He has put into all His creation; therefore it
> is free to trace out His designs and humbly to
> follow His ways.[114]

Behind the transformationist pattern of life and thought lies a perception of undivided divine sovereignty. Unlike the dualist, who distinguishes manners of divine government appropriate to heavenly and earthly dominions, the conversionist regards God in Christ and Christ in God as the ruler of every human work and phase of culture. This radical view has not always been pursued to its logical conclusion. Dualistic elements are discernible, for example, in Augustinian and Calvinist insistences that only some people are brought to a life of glory.[115] But these instances represent departures from the conversionist stance. What made Maurice "the most consistent of conversionists" in Niebuhr's judgment was the fact that he held fast to the principle that Christ is king and rejected every dualistic tendency.[116] For Maurice, the universality and power of Christ's reign remains undiminished by doctrines of double predestination.

This resolution of the basic theological polarities leads to the belief that God is creating, judging, and reconciling the world in one undivided action. For the transformationist, integrity means adequacy to a revelation which transforms the believer's vision of the world. Intelligibility means adequacy to the believer's transformed experience of the world. Thus, for Augustine as for Calvin and Maurice, religious language is primarily the interpretation of every phase of existence under the lordship of Christ. Its basic

119

business is to indicate how all reality is related to the supremely good power by which all things come to be, are governed, and are redeemed, despite the mundane facts of crossed purposes and evil. In short, theology offers a redescription of human existence ruled by the God who acts to create, govern, and redeem that is distinct from other interpretations.

Like the synthesist, the conversionist recognizes important ways in which cultural forms of discourse make positive contributions to a theological interpretation of all things in relation to God. What distinguishes the conversionist's understanding of theological discourse from that of the synthesist is his insistence that sin has important epistemological consequences. Reasoned, philosophical interpretations of human life cannot be synthesized with revelation because they are skewed by the faith in self that lies behind them. On the one hand, convictions about creation and redemption prevent the conversionist from consigning the insights of reason and revelation to different spheres or kingdoms. On the other, his conviction about the radical nature of sin prevents him from identifying any particular cultural reason as an indispensable presupposition for intelligent Christian faith. Thus, the conversionist tends to conceive a pattern for theology that differs from those of the dualist and the synthesist.

With respect to theological discourse, the belief in the possibility for a renewal of cultural institutions becomes the conviction that reasoned interpretations may be transformed into earthen vessels for the intelligent communication of the Christian vision. This can be done if reasoned interpretations are placed within the perspective of context defined by Christ's lordship. Thus, the writer of the gospel of John is able to use Hellenistic ideas about Logos, knowledge, truth, and eternity by interpreting them through Christ.[117] Augustine borrows from Platonists in order to describe the appropriate orientation of people toward divine things, and Calvin finds admirable discourses on justice in the Latin Stoics.

The conversionist uses cultural reason in order to interpret and describe the world. But he reinterprets and redescribes this world under God in light of the historically particular revelation in Christ. His theological statements reflect a tension between general cultural discourse and specifically religious symbols. On the one hand, he makes use of cultural terms

120

and insights in order to describe human existence. On
the other, he places this description in a frame of reference ordered by a historically particular revelation
of divine activity and, thereby, alters its significance. He is bound to attempt comprehensive statements
of doctrine because the universal lordship of Christ
charges him to seek a catholic vision. At the same
time, he is bound to look upon all his theological
statements as imperfect and provisional, since they
are the works of a self tempted by sin whose finite
mind draws upon a reasoning that is part of the
temporal order.

          This dynamic arrangement is threatened by temp-
tations toward radicalism and dualism. The writers of
John's Gospel and the Letter to Diogenetus endorse a
separatist notion of the church because they fail to
connect the new life of the Christian community with
a hope for the conversion of the whole world. [118]
Augustine, Calvin, and Edwards fall into eschatological
dualism by allowing their radical understanding of sin
to take priority over convictions about the goodness of
creation and Christ's lordship. We may add that some
conversionists have been tempted in the direction of
synthesis and accommodation to identify the Christian
life with a specific ecclesiastical order and the intelligent presentation of doctrine with seventeenth century reason. Each of these temptations, of course, may
also affect a writer's understanding of theological
discourse.

          Niebuhr finds fault with transformationists
only where they depart from the inner logic of the conversionist pattern. By contrast, he criticizes the fundamental assumptions and logic of radicals, cultural
Christians, synthesists, and dualists. Thus, even
apart from the transformationist bent of his earlier
works, an examination of <u>Christ and Culture</u> indicates
that Niebuhr prefers the <u>conversionist pattern.</u> [119]

Theory and Practice

          For Niebuhr, the types fail to give a defini-
tive answer to the problem of Christ and culture.
Theology, or the theoretical reflection of Christians
about God and the world, does not determine the believer's answer to the problem of Christianity. To
give <u>the</u> Christian answer at the level of theory, we
would have to assume that we occupy the final place in
the church and its history. [120] To do so would be to usurp
the lordship of Christ. [120]

Clearly, Christians continue to act, and, says Niebuhr, the way a believer resolves contemporary issues will implicitly or explicitly contain his or her "final" answer.[121] Some have even found reasons to radicalize the disjunction between theory and practice. Søren Kierkegaard exposes the "monstrous illusion" that Christianity is something that can be known. In fact, he says, it can only be lived, since practical decisions are irreducibly personal and freely made in the moment.[122]

To radicalize the disjunction between the tentativeness of theory and the finality of practice in this way threatens not only the relevance of Niebuhr's typology, but also of the entire theological enterprise. It is roughly equivalent to the claim that theological knowledge about God and the world cannot inform, much less determine, practical Christian living. Niebuhr himself admits a disjunction of sorts between thought and action but seems unwilling to make it total. He agrees with Kierkegaard that becoming a Christian is an arduous affair of constant repentance made all the more difficult by the soul's meagre power to believe.[123] He agrees also that practical decisions are made in freedom by a believing subject in the present moment on the basis of what is true for him.[124] But to reduce Christian life to isolated subjectivity is not only to affirm personal freedom and to acknowledge a disjunction between thought and action. It is to construe the continuity between believers and the tradition in a highly idiosyncratic fashion that threatens the integrity of Christian life.

Like Kierkegaard, Niebuhr believes that the fragmentary nature of the believer's faith and knowledge sometimes issues in a failure of nerve. Rather than face the inner struggle and anxiety of authentic decision, Christians often invest creeds, history, codes of behavior, and institutions with absolute authority. They frustrate the transcendent reference of Christian living.[125] But Niebuhr also insists that mature believers can make decisions, aware that their faith and knowledge are fragmentary, without confusing their relative judgments with the absolute Christ.[126] Faith in the God who corrects evil and forgives sin enables believers to make practical decisions informed by their admittedly partial faith and partial knowledge.

If Niebuhr recognizes that decisions in faith are personal and made in the moment, he also insists that they have social and historical dimensions.

Kierkegaard's abstract existentialism neglects the
social character of Christ's promise and of human selfhood. Christ confronts people not with the self's isolated salvation, but with the salvation of the entire
human race to which the self belongs.[127] People decide
on the basis of what is true not only for themselves,
but also for a community of knowers to which they belong.[128] Selves confront Christ in the midst of a company of witnesses who point toward him and interpret
his presence. Moreover, this decidedly social encounter is also historical. The Christ who confronts
the self has a past and a future of relations to the
deciding self and to others. The self deciding in the
present moment remembers past experiences and knowledge
accumulated in converse with others and the Other.
Similarly, the self anticipates future occasions on
the basis of its social knowledge and experience.

Finally, Niebuhr believes that the decisions of
selves are made in freedom, but not in unqualified independence. They depend on circumstances and consequences beyond the self's control. It is possible to
believe that the self has been thrown into this matrix
of dependencies by chance, to affirm no discernible
pattern of meaning in the self's dependent context that
might help to direct its choices. For Niebuhr, however, one function of faith is to affirm that there is
an object loyal to the self which lends this context
coherence and meaning. Faith in this object become
value-center, whether it is self, nation, race, or
humanity, is the beginning of practical reasoning.
The promise of Christian faith is precisely that the
power selves call fate or chance is faithful and loyal
to all beings. What is irrational to the self's practical thought is the creation of faith in the trust-
worthiness of God by the crucifixion and betrayal of
the one who was utterly loyal to Him.[129] This faith in
the Determiner of Destiny is the beginning of the believer's practical reasoning. It enables Christians to
reinterpret the matrix of dependencies in which they
live and move as a unified context for decision that
directs personal freedom.

The Christian called upon to discern and respond to the universal action of God in every particular is aided by "consulting the charts his fathers
used when they set out on the same voyage he is continuing."[130] The types define answers to the problem
of Christ and culture "that recur so often that they
seem to be less the product of historical conditioning
than the nature of the problem itself and the meaning

of its terms."[131] These answers train the believer
in the interpretative key and scale of the Christian
charts. They review alternative ways that Christians
have envisioned the experiential context for practical
decision. They display the major patterns in which
the interpretative images of the faith have been arranged to achieve intelligible redescriptions of lived
experience.[132]

    No theoretical investigation can determine the
decisions of believers. But the decisions of believers
can be informed by theoretical inquiry.

> If this is the conclusion of our study--that
> the problem of Christ and culture can and must
> come to an end only in a realm beyond all study
> in the free decisions of individual believers
> and responsible communities--it does not follow
> that it is not also our duty to attend to the
> ways in which other men have answered and
> answer the question, and to ask what reason-
> ing accompanied their free, relative and
> individual choices.[133]

Though there is no smooth transition from experience to
theory, the believer does not decide how to respond in
the present without consulting what collaborators and
corroborators have thought and done. Nor does he decide without consulting how companions think and act.
To do so would be to jeopardize the integrity of Christian living and, finally, also its intelligibility.
Nor does the believer decide upon a form of life by
consulting what others do and have done without reference to his own experience. To do so would be to live
out of a fossilized tradition, to negate the intelligibility of faith and, finally, also its integrity.

    Thus, to favor a transformationist or any other
Christian vision is not merely to accept a theoretical
conclusion, but also to adopt a practical outlook.
There is little reason to assume that Christian ways
of life emerge in a purely inductive fashion from lived
experience, and even less reason to believe that they
are simply deduced from theological premises.

    Like the other patterns which dominate the
church of the center, transformationism supports a
vision that mediates the meanings and values of faith
to believers who participate in the world. Confirmation for this or any other Christian vision is to be
found in life-performance.[134] Theologically, this life

performance can be supported for trinitarian reasons. Since the Redeemer is also the Creator and Governor of culture, nothing less than a pattern of practical life and logic that engages the reason and order of social life can claim to be fully in his service.

The difference between a transformationist pattern and other mediating alternatives is that God is perceived to act in culture both as Judge and Redeemer. Because God judges cultures, the conversionist cannot synthesize Christian faith with any specific society, but is led to criticize cultural values and practices. Because God acts to redeem in culture, the conversionist does not limit responsive social activity to criticism and restraint of evil, but also pursues good through cultural values and institutions.

This dual impulse imitates the double movement in Christ from the world to God and from God to the world.[135] It commits the believer to a dynamic arrangement of loyalties to Christ and to culture. If he cannot reject social loyalties, neither can he embrace them uncritically or balance them smoothly with his Christian commitment.

[1] CC, p. 4.

[2] Ibid., pp. 9-10.

[3] Ibid., p. 10.

[4] Ibid., p. 2.

[5] Ibid., p. 12.

[6] Ibid., p. 11.

[7] Ibid., p. 12.

[8] Ibid., p. 13.

[9] Ibid., p. 14.

[10] Ibid., pp. 16-19, 27.

[11] Ibid., p. 28.

[12] Ibid.

[13] Ibid., pp. 28-29.

[14] Ibid., p. 32.

[15] Ibid.

[16] Ibid., pp. 9, 33-39.

[17] Ibid., pp. 34-35. Despite culture's humanistic emphasis, however, no culture is humanistic in the broad sense. Instead, there are only particular societies, and each tends to regard itself as the center and source of value. So, for example, the very future and hope of civilization is often thought to be borne by particular societies and nations.

[18] Ibid., p. 10.

[19] Ibid., p. 40.

[20] See Ibid., pp. 76-82, 110-115, 117-119. Niebuhr examines difficulties associated with the Christ against culture type with reference to the way its representatives construe relations between reason and revelation, sin and holiness, law and grace, and

Jesus Christ or God the redeemer and God the creator and governor of nature. He reviews objections to the Christ of culture answer with reference to interpretations of reason and revelation, grace and law, the relations between persons of the Trinity, and the view of sin offered by its major representatives. The three typical answers offered by more orthodox Christians are in substantial agreement about Jesus' relation to God or his sonship, the use of human intelligence in obedience to God, the universality and radicality of sin, and the relation between grace and law.

[21]I am especially indebted to my colleague at Union Theological Seminary in Virginia, Charles M. Swezey, for enriching my understanding of Christ and Culture and for pointing out the four fundamental motifs in Niebuhr's presentation.

[22]There is, of course, even less reason to think that they begin with notions concerning the public currency of religious and theological discourse.

[23]CC, pp. 43-44.

[24]See Ibid., pp. 93, 167-168. The second century gnostic Marcion and the nineteenth century liberal theologian Friedrich Schleiermacher are examples. According to Niebuhr, Marcion may be associated with the gnostics and the "of culture" position as well as with the "against culture" group which founds sects that separate from the church and are marked by religious asceticism. On balance, however, Niebuhr locates Marcion in the paradox or dualist camp. The Schleiermacher of the Speeches on Religion, says Niebuhr, represents the Christ of culture type, but he does not so evidently represent it in The Christian Faith.

[25]Ibid., p. 231.

[26]Ibid., p. 45.

[27]Ibid., p. 46.

[28]Ibid., p. 51.

[29]Ibid., pp. 58-59.

[30]Ibid., p. 63.

[31]Ibid., pp. 65-68.

[32]Ibid., p. 69.

[33]Ibid.

[34]Ibid., p. 77.

[35]Ibid., p. 83.

[36]Ibid., p. 103.

[37]Ibid., p. 85.

[38]Ibid., p. 89.

[39]Ibid., pp. 91-92.

[40]Ibid., p. 94.

[41]Ibid., p. 95.

[42]Ibid., pp. 110-111.

[43]Ibid., p. 113.

[44]Ibid., p. 112.

[45]Barth, CD, I/1, pp. 4, 14.

[46]Ibid., pp. 6-10, 28, 29.

[47]Ibid., III/4, pp. 169-172, 176-183, 331. At
this point, it is important to remember Niebuhr's cau-
tion that no theologian entirely fits an ideal type.
This is especially true of Karl Barth. The only claims
made here are 1) that Barth's theology closely follows
Niebuhr's description of the anitcultural position on
the relation between reason and revelation, 2) that
this leads Barth to articulate a particular notion of
intelligibility in theology and the nature of theological discourse to which, 3) he does not always
stringently adhere.

[48]CC, p. 40.

[49]Ibid., p. 118.

[50]Ibid.

[51]Ibid.

[52]Ibid., p. 119.

[53]Ibid., pp. 126-127.

[54]Ibid., pp. 120-121.

[55]Ibid., pp. 121, 125; Origen, On First Principles, trans. G.W. Butterworth (New York: Harper and Row, 1966), pp. 15-28.

[56]CC, p. 124.

[57]Ibid., p. 131.

[58]Ibid., p. 129.

[59]Ibid., p. 132; Thomas Aquinas, Summa Theologica, trans. Fathers of the English Dominican Province, 2 vols. (New York: Benziger Brothers, n.d.), I-II, 109, 5.

[60]Aquinas, Summa, I-II, 109, 1-5.

[61]CC, pp. 135-136.

[62]Aquinas, Summa, I-II, 91, 2.

[63]CC, p. 135.

[64]Aquinas' extensive discussion of reasons for the necessity of the divine law appears in Summa, I-II, 91-93.

[65]CC, p. 70.

[66]Etienne Gilson, Reason and Revelation in the Middle Ages (New York: Charles Scribner's Sons, 1938), p. 84.

[67]Aquinas, Summa, II-II, 9.

[68]Gilson, Reason and Revelation in the Middle Ages, p. 83; Thomas Aquinas, Siger of Brabant, Bonaventure, On the Eternity of the World, trans. Cyril Vollert, Lottie Kendzierski, Paul M. Bryne, Mediaeval Philosophical Texts in Translation, no. 16 (Milwaukee: Marquette University Press, 1964), pp. 50, 51, 58-59.

[69]CC, p. 143.

[70]Ibid., p. 145.

[71]Ibid., p. 146.

[72] Ibid., p. 152; Aquinas, _Summa_, II-II, 9, 3.

[73] Aquinas, _Summa_, I, 19-22; III, 1, 2.

[74] CC, p. 131.

[75] Ibid., p. 147.

[76] Ibid., pp. 149-150.

[77] Ibid., pp. 159-167.

[78] Ibid., pp. 170-171.

[79] Ibid., p. 180.

[80] Ibid., p. 151.

[81] Ibid.

[82] Ibid., pp. 152-154.

[83] Ibid., p. 152.

[84] Ibid., p. 156.

[85] Ibid., pp. 156-157.

[86] Ibid., p. 172.

[87] All citations from the writings of Martin Luther are from Martin Luther, _Luther's Works_, gen. ed. Jaroslav Pelikan and Helmut Lehmann, 56 vols. (St. Louis: Concordia Publishing House, 1955-1976) hereafter cited as _Works_. See Luther, "Lectures on Romans," _Works_, 25:259.

[88] CC, p. 173.

[89] Ibid., p. 151.

[90] Luther, _Works_, 25:257.

[91] Ibid., 25:263.

[92] Luther, "The Freedom of A Christian," _Works_, 31:344.

[93] CC, p. 174.

[94] Ibid., p. 171.

[95] Luther, "Lectures on Galatians," _Works_, 26:5, 26, 34, 157, 173-174, 227-331; 31:376.

[96] CC, p. 185.

[97] Ibid.

[98] Ibid., pp. 188-189.

[99] Luther, _Works_, 25:313.

[100] CC, p. 189.

[101] Ibid., pp. 172, 187.

[102] Ibid., p. 188.

[103] Ibid.

[104] Ibid., p. 185.

[105] Ibid.

[106] Ibid., pp. 196-197.

[107] Ibid., p. 191.

[108] Ibid., p. 192.

[109] Ibid., pp. 194-196.

[110] Calvin, _The Institutes of the Christian Religion_, 20:253-254.

[111] CC, p. 223.

[112] Alec R. Vidler, _Witness to the Light: The Theology of F.D. Maurice_ (New York: Charles Scribner's Sons, 1948), pp. 36-37.

[113] Calvin's third use of the law is a classic example. See Calvin, _The Institutes of the Christian Religion_, 20:360-363.

[114] CC, pp. 214-215.

[115] Ibid., pp. 216-218.

[116] Ibid., p. 224.

[117] Ibid., pp. 196-197.

[118]Ibid., pp. 204-206.

[119]This indicates that Niebuhr's analysis is prejudiced by his transformationist viewpoint. Indeed, he settles upon preliminary definitions of Christ and culture that would be unacceptable from the viewpoints of radical and cultural Christians. But it seems that the only way to evaluate normative understandings of Christian faith is in light of another normative understanding. The observation that the extreme positions fail to duplicate the understanding of nature and grace expressed by trinitarian doctrine constitutes a criticism only if one accepts the orthodox doctrine of the Trinity. But criticism of orthodox trinitarianism has been one of the hallmarks of radical and cultural groups. There is nothing to prevent criticism of the conversionist stance from other points of view. Dualist Christians might criticize transformationists for holding a less than sufficiently radical doctrine of sin and so on. The typological analysis helps one to clarify important differences and similarities between the types and to anticipate criticisms that their representatives are likely to direct against each other. One may plausibly argue that a similar investigation written from another point of view would evaluate the types very differently.

[120]Ibid., p. 232.

[121]Ibid., pp. 233-235.

[122]H. Richard Niebuhr, "Søren Kierkegaard," Christianity and the Existentialists, ed. Carl Michalson (New York: Charles Scribner's Sons, 1956), pp. 28-36.

[123]Ibid., p. 41.

[124]CC, p. 241.

[125]"Søren Kierkegaard," pp. 35-36, 42.

[126]CC, p. 238.

[127]Ibid., pp. 244-245.

[128]Ibid., p. 245.

[129]Ibid., p. 254.

[130]"Is God in the War?" p. 954; KGA, p. 15.

131CC, p. 40.

132A similar relationship between interpretative categories of the religious community and the moral description of experience is suggested by Niebuhr in Waldo Beach and H. Richard Niebuhr, Christian Ethics: Sources of the Living Tradition (New York: Ronald Press, 1955), pp. 3-45. For Niebuhr, the Bible is a living tradition since the principles, symbols, and categories it presents illumine actual experience.

133CC, p. 233.

134Julian Hartt, Theological Method and Imagination (New York: Seabury Press, A Crossroad Book, 1977), pp. 43-44.

135CC, pp. 28-29.

CHAPTER VI

INTERPRETING CULTURE AND AGENCY

Niebuhr's transformationist stance is founded
on the conviction that faith in the sovereign Lord who
is active in all things as Creator, Governor, and Redeemer alters the believer's vision of the world. Were
this stance unable to make sense of contemporary life,
Niebuhr's theology would be incoherent. Not only
would it lack intelligibility in the modern world,
but it would also lack continuity with the thought
of Augustine, Calvin, and Maurice.

In Radical Monotheism, Niebuhr argues that the
faith in God made known through Jesus Christ adequately
interprets the loyalties of modern culture while less
radical faiths do not. This amounts to a theology of
culture which suggests that Christian faith is intelligible in the modern world. In The Responsible Self, he
interprets human moral life from a Christian point of
view.[1] His interpretation is broadly philosophical,
since it can be accomplished only with the aid of an
image which has emerged in modern culture. It amounts
to what Niebuhr calls "An Essay in Christian Moral
Philosophy," and suggests that an interpretation of
moral life that is intelligible in the modern world
can also have integrity to the biblical witness.

An Interpretation of Culture

The argument of Radical Monotheism and Western
Culture may be divided into three parts. In the first,
Niebuhr describes the task of theology and identifies a
common structure of human faith present in social relations. In the second, he argues that three forms of
faith, among them radical monotheism, emerge in western
culture and remain in constant conflict. Finally, he
describes this conflict in different arenas of cultural
activity and shows how radical faith in God enables a
unified vision of social life.

For Niebuhr, theology has a dual task.[2] It extends the relevance of believing in God, and it criticizes faith in relation to its object(s). As construction, theology develops the reasoning already present
in faith. Though it operates at a more abstract level,
theological construction begins with faith's apprehension of God and relates all things to it. As critique,
theology evaluates faith as a subjective attitude or
activity in relation to its objects. Here also,

participation in the life of faith is indispensable. Otherwise, the critic will fail to distinguish symbol and meaning as well as faith's genuine and spurious expressions.

Niebuhr's interpretation of culture is theology in both senses. It extends the reasoning of faith in God about the social environment, and it criticizes other human faiths with reference to their objects. This analysis is possible because faith is present not only in religion, but also in all social activities.[3] Thus, for example, the citizen who goes to war for his country regards the nation as a center of value. He has confidence that it is meaningful to be a member of the national community. Because the nation has been good to him, because it has faithfully valued him, the soldier takes it as his cause. Going to war expresses his fidelity to the nation as a cause for which he lives and also may die.

Though the objects to which people commit themselves are various, "the spirit of fidelity . . . is always the same."[4] A common structure of faith "is apparently universal or general enough to be widely recognized."[5] Following Leo Tolstoy and especially Josiah Royce, Niebuhr maintains that human faith is a double movement of trust and loyalty. It is a self's fundamental attitude and action of trust in and loyalty to certain realities apprehended as sources of meaning and value. The forms or styles of life that people adopt express their faith in some object of value made cause. If faith and its object or god go together, so do faith and a self's basic orientation or form of life.[6]

Theology examines diverse faiths with reference to their objects, since different faiths and the forms of life they engender can only be understood in light of their different centers of value. Faith in the God who is active as Creator, Governor, and Redeemer is one of the basic orientations present in western culture. The theologian compares it with others to clarify its meaning and examines reasons for the failure of faiths which attach themselves to less than ultimate objects.[7]

For Niebuhr, three broad types of faith are discernible in western society. Each is characterized by the class or kind of reality people trust, by the specific strain of loyalty or commitment elicited by the trusted reality, and by the particular form of life it engenders.[8] Thus, a henotheist takes the social group as the source and center of all that is good, including his own value. As his cause, the society elicits his loyalty to its continuation, power, and glory.[9] Persons and things are thought to have worth to the extent that they serve the ends of society and are loyal to it. The diverse activities of people, as well as their lesser confidences and loyalties, can be arranged beneath the unifying umbrella of henotheistic faith in the larger society.

Niebuhr owes this portrait in part to Emil Durkheim.[10] The individual is dependent on society as it is not dependent on him. At precisely this point, the henotheist perceives himself to be in touch with a valued reality that transcends his own life. His faith has its holy days and cultic objects, and it comes to practical expression in a tendency to define merit or guilt in relation to social authority and to live in obedience to social norms.

Nationalism is a prime example. For the nationalist, national welfare and survival become the supreme ends of life. Right and wrong are defined by the sovereign will of the nation. Cultural activities, like science, education, art, and religion, "are valued by the measure of their contribution to national existence" as are social companions.[11]

As a type, henotheism is polymorphic. Niebuhr refers to Marxist faith in the proletariat, humanist faith in civilization, and sectarian faith in the cause of the religious group as non-nationalist variants.[12] Binding norms and authorities may be those of a tribe, race, nation, class, or religious association. The important thing is that they remain the standards of a closed or limited society which point beyond themselves to the society itself or to its exclusive cause as the supreme object of value.

Social faith may be broken by internal conflicts, natural disasters, or external encounters with more powerful groups.[13] When henotheism fragments, the sense that the self is important because it belongs to an enduring community is replaced by the feeling that it must prove its worth by engaging in a plurality of activities.[14] The result is what Niebuhr calls polytheism.

Polytheists place their confidence in a series of unrelated value centers. In their search for self-worth, they serve a variety of causes connected only because the self chooses these rather than others. The objectivity of these values may be posited, or the question of their reality may be simply ignored. In either case, the individual and his society no longer have an inclusive vision or point of reference against which to judge relative values and competing ideals. Society degenerates into a loose assemblage of associations and special interests. The self becomes a bundle of compartmentalized functions and activities. Now devotion to family, now economic success, now nurture of the arts, now pursuit of knowledge, now increase in religion provide the causes for which the self labors and lives.

Radical monotheism, the third form of faith present in western culture, points to "the principle of being itself" as the sole value center. Truly radical faith, says Niebuhr, refers "to no one reality among the many but to the One beyond the many, whence the many derive their being, and by participation in which they exist."[15] It identifies the principle of being, or the power by which all things come to be, with the principle of value, or the power by which all things have worth.

The henotheist has confidence in his worth because he participates in a closed society. He judges the worth of persons and things by their participation in and contributions to the closed society. The polytheist proves his worth by contributing to a plurality of causes and judges the worth of others by their contributions to a similar variety of gods. For the radical monotheist, however, whatever participates in existence is good.[16] He is assured of his worth simply because he exists.

This faith is radical because its scope is universal. It elicits loyalty to the entire community of being.

> The neighbor is no longer the member of a
> closed society whose citizens support each
> other by rendering mutual service, but any
> member of that community of which the uni-
> versal God is the head.[17]

A form of life emerges in which there is no privileged or "in-group." Instead, moral requirements are extended to cover relations within the universal community of all existents. [18]

Expressions like "principle of being" and "center of value" have led some readers of Niebuhr's text to a metaphysical misunderstanding of radical monotheism. No less heralded a contemporary than Jürgen Moltmann decries Niebuhr as a theologian who tries to understand Christian faith from a metaphysical starting point.[19] For Niebuhr, however, the identification of the principle of being with the principle of value is not, in the first instance, a philosophical accomplishment. Rather, it is the legacy of faith's confession which identifies the Creator with the Redeemer. Trust in the principle of being is not deduced from a prior ontology which establishes the unity of the realm of being and its source in a single transcendent power. Loyalty to being as the source of value is not deduced from a philosophical proof of the goodness of the natural order.

> Believing man does not say first, "I believe
> in a creative principle," and then, "I believe
> that the principle is gracious, that is good
> toward what issues from it." He rather says,
> "I believe in God the Father, Almighty, maker
> of heaven and earth." This is a primary state-
> ment, a point of departure and not a deduction.
> In it the principle of being is identified with
> the principle of value and the principle of
> value with the principle of being.[20]

For the author of <u>Radical Monotheism</u> as much as for the author of <u>The Meaning of Revelation</u>, theology begins with the language of faith. The confessional language of believers indicates that faith has to do with relations between selves and that its object is a faithful, truthful Person.[21] The integrity that is fundamental in revelation as an event which elicits personal confidence in the ultimate environment and calls for the loyalty of selves to the universal cause is the "principle of personlike integrity."[22] But, the appropriate integration of self in the presence of the faithful Person is a response in loyalty and confidence to the faithful One who is present in all events.[23] This response requires a reasoning faith which looks for recurrent patterns in the midst of initially novel experiences. Thus, our theoretical minds are also engaged and look "for recurrent patterns of behavior or enduring structures or permanent relations or abstract universals."[24] Theology, therefore, tries to define <u>ideas</u> of God and <u>forms</u> of faith.[25] As the disciplined development of reasoning faith, it necessarily deploys both personal and impersonal symbols. Terms like "principle of being," "principle of value," and "the One beyond the many" are impersonal expressions of the rational effort to understand God and his relation to the world that is characteristic of radical faith.[26] Admittedly, these impersonal categories are unable to express faith's irreducibly personal dimension, but, then, they are not intended to replace faith's personal symbols. Their function is to point intellectually toward what believing selves acknowledge as "Thou" and thereby contribute to a more comprehensive vision of all things related to God.[27]

For Niebuhr, the process of fashioning an intelligible and comprehensive vision which combines concretely personal and abstractly rational elements is true to scripture. Nothing less is required of a theology that has integrity to the biblical witness.

In the story of Biblical faith the revelation of the First Person was the beginning of a process of coherent reasoning in faith for which no event in nature or in social history could be dismissed as accidental, arbitrary, unintelligible, or disconnected, as product of some independent power . . . . Confidence in cosmic faithfulness held to the assurance that there was one self-consistent intention in apparent evil as well as in apparent good though how it was present often remained unfathomed.[28]

A metaphysical misreading of Niebuhr's text fails to grasp that, for Niebuhr, faith's language is primary. It also fails to discern the biblical root of his explicitly trinitarian doctrine of God. Revelation rather than metaphysics is the starting point, and faith's apprehension of a personal, trinitarian diety related to all things informs the radical monotheist's perspective.

According to Niebuhr, theoretical ideas of the One beyond the many and of universal loyalty emerge in Greek philosophy. But we encounter the incarnation of radical faith, or its concrete expression in total human life, only in the history of the Jewish people.[29] Certainly, the history of Israel is filled with strife between radical faith and social loyalties. "But monotheism is expressed in all activities and the conflict about it takes place in connection with each activity."[30] Human relations, whether familial, economic, cultic, political, or international are transformed

140

into covenantal relations. They become faith relations of promise making and promise keeping.

"Jesus Christ represents the incarnation of radical faith to an even greater extent than Israel."[31] Here, confidence in the transcendent One as well as loyalty to his kingdom of all existents are focused in the prism of a personal life. The dual faithfulness to God and to companions which characterizes the structure of covenantal friendship is concentrated in Jesus' person, teaching, and example.

> The word of God as God's oath of fidelity became flesh in him in the sense that he was a man who single-mindedly accepted the assurance that the Lord of heaven and earth was wholly faithful to him and to all creatures, and who in response gave wholehearted loyalty to the realm of being. [32]

For Niebuhr, three notes of revelation recur in God's self-disclosure to Moses, his revelation to the prophets, and his revelation in Jesus Christ. First, God is nothing less than being. He is Creator, the source of all that is, or the principle of being. Second, the Creator is valuer and savior. Being or the power of being is also the Governor and Redeemer. Third, the disclosure "that the ultimate principle of being maintains and re-establishes worth" challenges people to make God's cause their own. Revelation elicits loyalty to all creation or to the realm of being to which God himself is loyal.[33]

Properly understood, the idea or form of radical monotheism is a further development of Niebuhr's transformationist stance. Whether radical faith is always present to humanity in hiddenness or originally made known in revelation, it comes to explicit expression only through concrete incarnation in our history. These conscious expressions give reasoning faith a starting point from which to construct a vision of the world in relation to the God who is active in apparent evil as well as apparent good, who enables and requires moral seriousness in all aspects of life, and who acts through all events in nature and social history. A theological analysis of culture guided by the trinitarian identification of the principle of being with the principle of value participates in this faithful reasoning and contributes to a more comprehensive vision of all things in relation to the God who acts.[34]

The conflict between the forms of faith is discernible in western religion, politics, and science. Following Rudolf Otto, Niebuhr understands piety as awe in the presence of the holy. This powerful but inchoate response to transcendent reality receives direction and organization from ritual, doctrine, and tradition that are influenced by one or another of faith's forms.

In its primitive guise, for example, polytheism ascribes holiness to a variety of natural objects, while its contemporary expressions direct religious appreciation toward varied works of humanity, like music, art, and technology. Henotheism directs the sense of the holy toward symbols of the closed society. Emperors become demigods. Flags and seals of public office become cultic objects. By contrast, radical monotheism redirects our sense of the holy toward the One beyond the many. Consequently, the numinous aura of mundane objects invested with divinity is broken. The constructive counterpart of this secularization is the sanctification of all things. No longer regarded as divine, natural objects and phenomena become parts of God's creation. No longer deified, society becomes a historical community called forth by God that exists under his rule.

How difficult a radically monotheistic reorganization of the holy is can be seen from the history of western religion. Here, we constantly encounter efforts to ascribe sacredness to some special community and to divide it from the profane.

A holy church is separated from a secular world; a sacred priesthood from an unhallowed laity; a holy history of salvation from the unsanctified course of human events; the sacredness of human personality, or of life, is maintained along with the acceptance of a purely utilitarian valuation of animal existence or of non-living being. [35]

Conflict among the forms of faith appears even in avowedly monotheistic religions. The doctrine of redemption may be set forth in a universalist form or in a henotheistic context that reserves salvation for some special enclave of being. [36] Judaism is periodically tempted by henotheistic loyalty to the closed society. In Christianity, henotheism tends to take either a church-centered or Christ-centered form. For some, the church itself may be elevated as the

142

guarantor of salvation or as God's sole agent in the world. "To have faith in God and to believe the church become one and the same thing."[37] For others, Jesus is made the absolute center of confidence and loyalty, and piety substitutes the lordship of Christ for the lordship of the God to whom Christ points. Christocentrism collapses the Trinity into the second Person, transmutes theology into christology, and supports an exclusive ecclesiasticism which regards the church as the locus and privileged bearer of its special god.[38]

From Niebuhr's viewpoint, Judaism and Christianity present a dominant drive toward the total transformation of life in conflict with lesser loyalties.[39] Each faces the dilemma of intensity and universality in a different way. Judaism tends to sacrifice universality by an intensive reorganization of cultural life which leads people to substitute henotheistic allegiance to the group for their faith in the One God. Christianity tends to sacrifice intensity by a universal acceptance of all people which uncritically neglects their many cultural loyalties and reforms only their spiritual lives.[40]

For our purposes, the important point is that transformationism, which informs Niebuhr's idea of radical monotheism, supports an adequate interpretation of western religion. His interpretation is intelligible because it is adequate to what we know about western religion from non-theological sources, e.g., the disciplines of history, philosophy, and social science. What Niebuhr says about religion from his perspective is understandable to those who are not religious. Also, his interpretation is more adequate to the biblical witness than henotheistic or polytheistic interpretations would be, unless one views the Bible as a record of life whose dominant thrust is to recommend allegiance to a closed society or to a variety of finite causes rather than to the universal, sovereign God.

As fidelity to a cause, faith is also prominent in western politics. The modern nation-state, says Niebuhr, represents itself as a society with a mission. It wins the loyalty of its citizens because it is loyal to a cause transcending itself, and "it presupposes the direct fidelity of its citizens to the transcendent cause."[41] Thus, the United States presents itself as a nation loyal to the cause of democracy, while the Soviet Union presents itself as a nation loyal to communism.[42] The loyalty of their citizens is claimed

143

on the one hand by the transcendent cause and on the
other, by the nation itself as representative of the
cause. 43

Henotheism emerges when the nation is immediately and exclusively identified with its cause, as
when the United States becomes synonomous with democracy and criticism of the nation in light of its democratic ideal ceases.   Polytheism is present when political decisions are made solely by a coalition of special interest groups devoted to partial causes.   Nevertheless, political loyalties are also qualified by
monotheistic convictions.   Thus, for example, the
limitation of power in America and the continued
practice of balancing powers

> have their origins in the need of finding com-
> promise among rival claimants to authority if
> national loyalty is to be supreme; but also in
> the conviction that ultimate power belongs
> only to God and that in the nature of things,
> according to the constitution of the universal
> commonwealth as it were, finite power is ac-
> tually limited and works destructively if it
> is not guarded against the constant temptation
> to make itself infinite, totalitarian, and
> godlike. 44

Niebuhr uses the democratic belief in human
equality to illustrate his interpretation.   The "self-
evident truth" that "all men are created equal" is
really a statement of faith, a pledge subject to ever
renewed commitment.   The pledge entails the monotheistic conviction that people are related to a common
center of value.   They have equal worth because they
are equally related to the source of existence.   In
each new decision about the application of this principle, the struggle between monotheism and its rivals
re-emerges. 45

The doctrine of equality sustains attacks which
insist that people are not equal in light of their contributions to the life of the species, or to the life
of reason, or to the life of the nation.46   For the
most part, these attacks express a pluralistic faith.
"Men are unequal in their relations to all the limited
gods, all the limited centers of value, and in the contributions they make to all the exclusive causes."47
Their worth in one relation does not coincide with
their worth in others.   Thus, the great scientist may
be a criminal; the superb physical specimen a dunce.

144

Pluralistic faith can only organize limited coalitions devoted to partial causes that are useful within a larger framework of justice as equal opportunity. It can organize no commonwealth, and for this reason, fails to offer political society "any real alternative to the dogma of equality."[48]

Other attacks express henotheistic loyalties. Racists reject the doctrine of equality in light of their faith in the supremacy of a particular race. Nationalists also qualify the dogma by setting it within the context of their social loyalty. They recognize the right of citizens to equal treatment, but they deny this right to foreigners.[49]

The main point is that Niebuhr's perspective supports an adequate interpretation of western politics. It successfully interprets what we know about the facts of authority, constitutionalism, pluralism, racism, and nationalism in western culture. In short, Niebuhr's interpretation of politics is at least understandable to those who do not harbor monotheistic convictions.

The conflict of faiths is also discernible in western science. Something like the radical faith we find in religion and politics is present in the faithfulness of the scientific community to non-scientists and in the confidence which guides scientific inquiry. Investigators have honored the right of persons to the whole truth by accurately communicating their specialized knowledge to the wider human community. Of course, this expression of radical faith sustains henotheistic challenges. When scientific inquiry is set in the context of nationalism, there is pressure to regard its value exclusively in relation to the national cause. Secrecy and deception may thwart the obligation to tell the truth. Also, research may be carried on in the context of a henotheism of the scientific community which regards scientific truth as the only true good. The resultant scientism values persons and things only insofar as they contribute to the quest for scientific knowledge.

Radical faith is present also in the convictions which guide scientific inquiry. A self-critical attitude struggles to overcome the human tendency to begin with ourselves as the center of value in order to focus disinterested attention on the object under investigation.[50] Moreover, scientific skepticism toward all claims to absolute knowledge and significance seems analogous, says Niebuhr, to the iconoclasm and relativization which accompanies radical faith in other cultural activities.[51]

More positively, radical faith seems present in the loyalty of scientists to the cause of universal knowledge and the confidence with which pure science approaches anything and everything as potentially meaningful.[52] Science appears to move with the confidence that "whatever is, is worthy of attention," even when phenomena challenge accepted theory. In this sense, the investigator carries on his inquiry with "universal intent." He does not search for relations which hold true only for some people, but tries to integrate his findings with a set of universal relations. Carried on in this fashion, says Niebuhr, western science takes its place alongside religion and politics guided by universal loyalty.

For our purpose, it is notable that Niebuhr's perspective enables an intelligible account of yet another aspect of modern culture. His interpretation of modern science is understandable to those who are acquainted with the history of scientific inquiry in the west and its relations to other cultural interests and communities, even if they do not share his radical faith. Moreover, henotheistic interpretations of scientific inquiry as an instrument of national glory and polytheistic interpretations of it as an end in itself are less than adequate to the broad purposes and objectives of science as a vocation in modern culture.

When these accounts of religion, politics, and science are regarded as a whole, a unified vision of contemporary life begins to emerge. This vision is adequate to the main facts of modern experience but also reinterprets them theocentrically. It admits that diverse cultural spheres have different proximate objects or purposes, e.g., the holy, the commonwealth, scientific knowledge; but it denies henotheistic hegemony to any single sphere. It recognizes that each area of cultural activity is guided by distinct principles but denies that these principles preside over a pluralistic cacaphony of disconnected activities. Instead, Niebuhr reinterprets the many loyalties of culture in the context of a universal faith, and in this setting, they are seen to point beyond themselves toward the One.

The interpretation of culture in Radical Monotheism is admittedly incomplete. But it might be

146

extended into other spheres, including the humanities.53
Indeed, a transformationist stance that claims integrity to the biblical perception of God active in all
events of nature and history and which also claims intelligibility in the modern world requires nothing less.

The Pattern of Responsibility

The Responsible Self continues this broad effort to construe human life theocentrically from a
Christian perspective. For Niebuhr, the Christian
life has its own form but is not discontinuous with
other ways of life. Christian ethics is the critical
examination of Christian life as a mode of human existence.54 The purpose of his "Essay in Christian Moral
Philosophy," then, is to form a prologue to that examination by undertaking a comprehensive interpretation
of human moral life.

This interpretation requires that the main
facets of our existence as agents be arranged in an illuminative pattern. However, selecting this pattern is
a major task of moral theology and an occasion for profound disagreements among theologians. Karl Barth, for
example, tries to dismiss all analogies, metaphors, and
symbols from Christian speech except Jesus Christ. Yet,
he is unable to interpret the meaning of Jesus Christ
without recourse to other symbols. Particularly in
speech about Christian ethics, he employs symbols like
commandment, law, obedience, and permission which are
biblical, though not exclusively so, and are hardly
distinctively Christian.55

For Niebuhr, the fact that Christians are unable to understand themselves in christocentric terms
alone raises an acute question. Is there a general
symbol which adequately interprets what we know about
divine activity through Christ and what we know about
our own activity in the modern world? If there is, it
will lay the foundation for an appropriate understanding
of ourselves as agents in relation to the God who acts.

There are at least three notable features of
Niebuhr's answer to this question. First, his Bible-informed approach differs from Barth's Bible-centered
position.56 Niebuhr's theology is broadly philosophical in the sense that the object to be investigated
is not the Christian life in isolation, but moral life
in general. Moreover, his organizing metaphor is drawn
from modern culture at large and is neither christocentric nor exclusively biblical.

147

Second, Niebuhr's approach differs from philosophical interpretations which claim to transcend any specific historical viewpoint.57 He both admits and affirms a perspective deeply conditioned by the presence of Jesus Christ in our history.58 He consciously tests his interpretative metaphor for its adequacy to distinctly Christian categories as well as to what we know about moral agency.59 Curiously, then, his Christian moral philosophy is "neither theological nor philosophical in the sense in which these terms are employed for the most part by professional workers in both groups." 60

Finally, Niebuhr's approach heightens the difficulty of selecting an appropriate organizing metaphor or pattern for interpreting human life. Culture no less than scripture is filled with images and symbols which might serve. To select critically, one needs to test each prospective image in light of what we know about human existence and what we know about God. But this requirement is problematic, since a detailed assessment of every prospective image is not possible.

Niebuhr's strategy is to argue that the metaphor of responsibility is more adequate theologically than two classical images which people have used to apprehend the form of their lives and to give shape to their actions.61 His argument is that the image of responsibility offers an interpretation that has integrity to the biblical witness and intelligibiity in the modern world. Though some may find this procedure unsatisfying, the consequence of failing to choose an organizing metaphor is to cut off the possibility of an adequate interpretation of human life. Theology seems to require that our critical impulses serve a wider constructive purpose.

What is important for our study is that Niebuhr's understanding of Christian moral philosophy is consistent with his transformationist stance and his radically monotheistic perspective. He marshalls general as well as more strictly theological reasons in support of his approach. He works from a particular point of view because value is relational and because no human observer escapes the conditions of history. He analyzes human moral life in general since, theologically considered, humanity's fundamental relation is to God and the sovereign God's relation to persons is not contingent on their acceptance or rejection of his presence.62

The same dual structure characterizes the argument in Niebuhr's chapter on "The Meaning of Responsibility." As is well known, he describes man-the-maker, man-the-citizen, and man-the-answerer as images which support alternative views of moral life and action. Each symbol represents a special experience through which all of experience may be interpreted. But man-the-answerer is more adequate to our ordinary experience as agents as well as to the biblical ethos.

For Aristotle, Thomas Aquinas, and other teleologists as well as those who employ means-ends reasoning and ask about the goals and purposes of cultural activities, the image of man-the-maker construes persons as artificers, technicians, or artists who fashion themselves and their social companions toward some end. Purposiveness answers the question "What shall I do?" by raising the prior question "What is my goal, ideal, or telos?"[63] Those who employ the political image of man-the-citizen living under law point out deficiencies of the teleological image. Persons, they say, must accept the physical and social natures which have been given to them. They cannot reject material which does not fit their ends. Again, who can plan his end? "Neither the material then with which we work nor the future building is under our control when the work is directed toward ourselves."[64] With respect to these things, we are more like citizens who rule themselves as being ruled than artists who give form to pliable materials.[65]

The symbol of the citizen comes to the fore in deontological philosophers and theologians who interpret self-existence in the midst of _mores_, commandments, and rules. In intellectual action, people not only direct inquiries toward a goal, but also carry on their inquiries under laws of logic and scientific method. In politics, they not only or perhaps even primarily seek the ends of order, peace, and welfare, but they adhere to the rule of justice. Deontology answers the moral question by raising the prior question "What is the law and what is the first law of my life?"[66]

For Niebuhr, debates between these two camps suggest that the quest for knowledge of ourselves is incomplete.[67] Man-the-answerer gives us a new symbol with which to understand our existence as agents.[68] In light of this image, all our actions are construed as having the character of responses or answers to actions upon us.[69]

The image of responsibility emerges with clarity only in the modern world, but it is "prefigured" by certain observations made by Aristotle and in Stoic ethics.[70] The idea of response guided by rational interpretation of circumstances and events plays a major role in Spinoza, and intimations of it are present in naturalism and Marxism. Responsibility answers the moral query in light of the prior question "What is going on?"[71] If teleology concerns itself with the good to be realized and deontology concerns itself with the right to be obeyed, responsibility is concerned with the fitting action, "the one that fits into a total interaction as response and as anticipation of further response."[72]

The image of man-the-answerer illumines dimensions of practical life which man-the-maker and man-the-citizen also successfully interpret. So far, a dead heat. But it also supports more adequate interpretations of social emergencies and personal suffering. Social crises, like the American Civil War and the Great Depression, indicate that

> the decision on which the future depends and
> whence the new law issues is a decision made
> in response to action upon the society, and
> this action is guided by interpretation of
> what is going on.[73]

Practical self-definition emerges more from response to challenge than from the pursuit of an ideal or adherence to ultimate laws. Again, from a teleological perspective, personal suffering is essentially meaningless, since it thwarts our purposive movement toward cherished goals. From a deontological viewpoint, suffering represents the intrusion into our lives of forces that do not follow our laws and therefore are without meaning. For responsibility, however, suffering is yet another sort of action impinging upon us which warrants interpretation and fitting reply, whether that reply be to change our goals and our rules or some other response.

This argument carries weight since the characters of agents and their communities are often fashioned in response to suffering and tragedy. Responses to the "D-days" of personal life help to shape the sort of persons we become, while responses of societies to wars and economic depressions decisively shape their ethos. Teleology and deontology, therefore, seem less than intelligible in light of what we know about the personal and social formation of human agents.

To this, Niebuhr adds a second argument about the integrity of the different images to theological categories that are prominent in the biblical ethos. Goal oriented thinking describes the ideal of Christian life in much Roman Catholic theology as the vision of God and in much liberal Protestantism as a harmony of beings in God's kingdom. But much that is in the Bible cannot be tailored to this pattern. Though he nowhere explicitly states it, one implication of Niebuhr's analysis of social tragedy and personal suffering is that a teleological scheme has difficulty accounting for God's ordering and judging activity in apparent evil. Also, man-the-maker seems unable to account for the eschatological transformation of all things in nature and history by God's redeeming grace.[74] Biblical portraits sometimes depict God acting with a purpose different from our own. These actions and the responses of believers to them, which conspicuously shape the biblical ethos, lie beyond the borders of teleological imagery.

Similarly, much that is biblical seems skewed or left out of account when the deontological image of human agency is used as the sole key to biblical interpretation. The legal interpretation of Christian ethics as an ethics of obedience misrepresents the polarity of law and gospel present in the biblical ethos and also the motif of God's eschatological action.

> Bultmann has transformed eschatology into existentialism in order to maintain an ethics of radical obedience; Barth has had to transform the law into a form of the gospel and the commandment into permission in order to reconcile the pecularity of gospel ethos with deontological thinking. There is doubtless much about law, commandment, and obedience in the Scriptures. But the use of this pattern does violence to what we find there.[75]

The character of biblical ethics can be more fully interpreted in light of the metaphor of responsibility. At critical junctures in the history of Israel and the early Christian communities, the basic question is "What is going on?" rather than "What is the goal?" or "What is the law?" Isaiah counsels his people to discern the action of God even in the actions of

Israel's enemies and to make a fitting reply. Jesus points "not the commander who gives laws but to the doer of small and mighty deeds."76 Importance is placed on interpreting the signs of the times and responding appropriately to the One who is active in everything that happens. Knowledge of God's end and purpose is important because it helps his people discern the meaning of what he is doing. Laws function more as guideposts that illumine what God is enabling and requiring his people to do than as rules to which obedience is required for its own sake.77

For our purposes, it is important to note that this dual argument addresses the dual requirements of integrity and intelligibility. But it is also critical to observe that Niebuhr frames the requirement of integrity to the biblical ethos in a way that is consistent with a transformationist stance and a radically monotheistic perspective. Man-the-maker seems inadequate to the biblical ethos because it is unable to interpret transformationist resolutions of sin-evil and goodness and nature and grace. Man-the-citizen fails to account for a transformationist resolution of law and gospel. Both classical symbols fail to interpret adequately the biblical and trinitarian perception of the God who is active in everything that happens, since they tend to direct attention toward a set of finite ideals, rules, or values rather than the One beyond the many. The clear implication is that human life can be interpreted with integrity to the Bible and intelligibility to the modern world only with the aid of an image which has emerged in the modern culture.

The argument of the first chapter anticipates the structure of the text as a whole. Niebuhr argues for the superior adequacy of the man-the-answerer to social, temporal, and contingent dimensions of practical life in chapters two through four. This amounts to the claim that the pattern of responsibility offers an interpretation of human life that is intelligible in the modern world. In the last chapter, he argues that responsibility is more adequate than the other patterns to the distinctly Christian understanding of human existence in sin and salvation. This amounts to the claim that man-the-answerer interprets human life in a way that has integrity to the biblical ethos.

According to Niebuhr, our attention has been directed toward the social character of human life in the modern period.78 This emphasis comes to the fore not only among existentialist philosophers like Martin

Buber, but also among social pychologists like George
Horton Cooley, George Herbert Mead, and Harry Stack
Sullivan.[79] The common claim is that the self comes
to be, human personality emerges, in interaction with
other selves.[80]

Theories of conscience indicate that the social
understanding of the self has a longer history in moral
philosophy than in other inquiries.[81] Immanuel Kant
remarks that while the function of conscience is a
business of man with himself, "yet he finds himself
compelled by his reason to transact it as if at the
command of another person."[82] For David Hume and Adam
Smith, conscience is not like being judged by another
person, but is the awareness of the actual approvals
and disapprovals of other people.[83] George Herbert
Mead believes that conscience is the experience of
oneself from the generalized standpoint of the social
group. Niebuhr goes a step further. The self, he
says, discerns constancies in its interactions with
social companions. The conscience is the self's awareness of the ethos of its society, "that is, of its
mode of interpersonal interactions."[84]

The image of man-the-maker, understanding himself primarily with reference to ideas and ideals, is
too individualistic to take adequate account of this
fundamentally social character of human selfhood.
Surely, ideals may be those of the social group, but
accountability, understood as the anticipation or expectation of replies by others to one's actions, has no
direct bearing on ideal standards. Because the teleol-
ogist measures himself and his accomplishments in relation to the ideal, his relation to other selves seems
secondary. The legal image of man-the-citizen appears
less individualistic, since laws are almost certainly
the standards of one's own community. Nevertheless,
for the deontologist, self-comparison, which is the
primary vehicle of self-knowledge, proceeds first with
reference to laws and only secondarily in relation to
other selves.

In light of responsibility, however, our moral
experience is primarily a matter of responses to the
interpreted actions of other agencies and powers.
These responses take place within the larger pattern
of constant interactions among a community of agents.
The self internalizes the interactive pattern of its
social ethos. This pattern enables the self to anticipate and expect the predictable actions of others
and so to respond with an eye toward their further

153

responses. At the same time that man-the-answerer
responds to any particular action, circumstance, or
event, he responds also to social companions. Thus,
the metaphor of responsibility offers an intelligible
interpretation of social selfhood in the modern world,
while man-the-maker and man-the-citizen seem unable to
account for what we know about social aspects of our
self-existence.

For Niebuhr, the responsible self exists in two
triadic relations.85 The first, which may be described
as the situation of speculative reason, has to do with
the interpretation of impersonal agencies and powers as
well as communication about them. As a social being
equipped with the images, categories, and theories of
its society, the self necessarily interprets impersonal
phenomena in a way that is partly dependent on social
reason and with an eye toward the responses of social
companions. Similarly, communication between selves
is ordinarily about some third thing with which both
social partners are in communication. The self's fitting reply to natural phenomena has an irreducible
social dimension, though it is partly independent from
society to the extent that the self can compare the
social reason or dominant pattern for interpretation
with its own experience.

The second triad, which may be distinguished
from the first for purposes of analysis but not separated in life, is the situation of selves bound together by loyalty to a cause. Examples of this situation are the loyalty of citizens and soldiers to each
other and to the cause of the nation, the loyalty of
fellow inquirers to each other and to the communal
cause of truth, and the loyalty of Christians to social
companions and to the cause of Jesus Christ.86

The cause present to us in all our responses to
companions has a dual character. It is something personal and marks off a mode of interpersonal interactions, but it also contains a reference to "something
that transcends it or to which it refers."87 Thus, a
democratic patriot in the United States carries on his
interactions with current companions as one who is also
in relation to a transcendent reference group, including Washingtons, Jeffersons, and Lincolns.88 By means
of this relation, he achieves a measure of independence
from his immediate companions. At the same time, this
reference group refers beyond itself to the cause of
democracy for which the community stands. Similarly,
students and faculty in a school are loyal not only to

each other, but also the cause of truth. This cause
may also be represented by a reference group of figures
who embody it.[89]

For Niebuhr, relations between self, neighbor,
Jesus Christ, and God are the greatest illustration
of this triad.[90] As I respond to companions in the
church, I am challenged to be faithful to the common
cause. That cause is represented by prophets and
apostles, but this reference group points beyond itself
to Jesus Christ. In a sense, Jesus Christ perfectly
embodies the pattern of interaction between self, God,
and neighbor that fits radical faith. At the same
time, he also points beyond himself toward God and invites our loyalty to the Creator.

For our purposes, the critical point is that
the pattern of responsibility can express radical monotheism. Now all our responses to social companions are
seen to be interrelated with responses to "God as the
ultimate person, the ultimate cause, the center of the
universal community."[91] For the radical monotheist,
"the process of self-transcendence or of reference to
the third beyond each third does not come to rest until
the total community of being has been involved."[92]
This leads us to the pattern of universal responsibility, of responsive life qualified by our interpretation
of all actions as taking place within a universe of
divine purpose, or by the universal spectator who regards all from a universal point of view.[93] Certainly,
teleology and deontology can also express the movement
toward the universal characteristic of radical faith,
but only in ways which leave important aspects of human
sociality out of account.

Niebuhr's argument about the adequacy of man-
the-maker, man-the-citizen, and man-the-answerer to our
existence as selves in time and history is similar.
Man-the-maker concentrates on the future time available
for realizing goals and ideals but has little room for
the significance of past and present.[94] For Immanual
Kant, the prime representative of formalist thinking,
practical reason "recognizes no distinction of time,"
while some existentialists regard man as the one who
defines himself in every present moment.[95] "Man-the-
citizen stands in the presence of a pure supertemporal
law valid for his reason as a pure, nontemporal
reason."[96]

By contrast, responsibility interprets the
self as a historical being who responds to a series of

155

timeful encounters. The self is aware of the present
moment when it is acted upon or "compresent with" a
not-self in threatening or promising form.[97] But the
past remains influential through memory, and the future
becomes influential through anticipation as the self
interprets and responds to present action. This pattern is also present in social life, where memories of
past war and depression, as well as expectations of
future scarcity or abundance, influence the responses
of nations and communities to present crises.

     From the viewpoint of radical faith, responsi-
bility also points to a religious dimension of our
temporal experience by raising the question of the
ultimate historical context "in which we respond and
by which we interpret all the specific actions upon
us."[98] If our interpretation of present events is modified in light of their larger temporal contexts, then
an understanding of their ultimate historical context
qualifies all of our interpretations and actions.
Where it is believed that origins were matters of
chance and that the future holds only the inevitable
encounter with decline and death, the life-histories of
individuals and empires are fitted into this context.
The result, says Niebuhr, is a defensive ethics of
survival, "of self-maintenance against threatening
power" present in the interactions of all things.[99]

     In this setting, the question of freedom is
the question of the self's ability to "achieve or re-
ceive a new understanding of its ultimate historical
context."[100] The great religions, and Christianity in
particular, enable the reinterpretation of this context
and, thus, qualify our inherited patterns of interaction. They challenge "the interpretative pattern of
the metahistory, within which all our histories and
biographies are enacted."[101] Different actions fit
into the history of creation and redemption than fit
into the context of accidental birth, decline, and inevitable death. If the transcendent social horizon of
radical faith is the universal community of being, its
ultimate temporal horizon is the universal history of
creation and redemption.

     The implication of Niebuhr's analysis of the
self in time and history is that teleology and deontology leave important dimensions of our timeful experience out of account. Furthermore, man-the-maker and
man-the-citizen offer truncated expressions of the
temporal horizon of radical faith, as when teleologists equate it with the open future and deontologists

identify it with the present moment. By contrast, responsibility affords an intelligible account of our historical existence as well as one which has integrity to Christian tradition.

Responsibility also supports an intelligible interpretation of the contingency of self-existence. According to Niebuhr, the self in encounter with others "finds itself absolutely dependent in its existence" and "inexplicably present in its here-ness and now-ness."[102] Biological and social sciences make it possible to identify and interpret many of the agencies and circumstances which act upon the self's body and mind. But none of these interpretations accounts for the fact that I have this body and this mind.

Again, with the aid of common sense and also historical studies, we note that our ideas, religious and otherwise, are formed in interaction with thinkers and writers in our era. Our thoughts are conditioned by our histories and the history of our society.

And yet after all this has been done two things remain uninterpreted: the radical action by which I was cast into this particular historical religious process, so that my interpretations and responses are directed toward particular challenges--in my case the challenges of the Christian religion; and the action by which I am.[103]

That common sense is aware of the sheer given-ness of self-existence seems clear from the child's question "Why I am I?", the statesman's wonder why he is matched in this hour with this nation, and the identity quests of uprooted moderns. Among philosophers, Martin Heidegger's discussion of the "thrownness" of our existence raises similar questions. Karl Heim refers to the category of fate, and Karl Jaspers and Gabriel Marcel also probe the mystery.

In light of response analysis, the main question raised by the contingency of self-existence is "How do I respond fittingly or appropriately to this most radical of all actions by which I am this self?" Our interpretation of and response to this primordial fact color our many responses to the actions, circumstances, and events of the finite world in which we are involved.[104] The responsible self is responsive to the singular givenness of self-existence in all of its responses to companions in existence.

One possible reaction to contingency, says
Niebuhr, is to try to ignore it or forget it. We
become absorbed in the plurality of momentary and
momentous actions upon us and ponder the fitting reply
of an American or a Christian to these lesser actions,
rather than the reply of a self to the radical action
by which it is. Another response, present in the East
more than the West, is to attribute self-existence to
a deluding power. "Self-consciousness, to use our
Western language, is the great illusion whence arise
the sorrows and cruelties of existence."105

For the Christian, these responses express
"faith in its negative form of distrust" toward existence and all of the finite existents which surround
the self.106 A Christian response to the radical action that thrusts us into existence is one made as
trust in the power of being. When we say that this
power is God, that the Creator is also the Redeemer,
we express the interpretation made in radical faith
that this power is good and beneficent.

In light of the metaphor of responsibility,
then, historic religions express interpretations of the
primordial action by which we are that illumine all of
life. Their interpretative skeins or patterns address
problems of self-knowledge as well as knowledge of the
moral order of the world. Thus, Christianity addresses
the subjective problem of the self's unity amidst the
plurality of relations in which it stands through the
trinitarian perception of God. To respond to the activity of the One in all our responses to the finite
agencies and systems in nature and history means "to
seek one integrity of self amidst all the integrities"
of various social roles and activities.107

Again, what is important for our purposes is
the way that Niebuhr's analysis of responsibility in
absolute dependence bears upon the requirements of
integrity and intelligibility. The image of man-the-
answerer adequately interprets what we know and apprehend about the contingency of self-existence in the
modern world. Moreover, it is amenable to the perspective of radical faith amidst the congeries of finite
agencies and so adequate to the trinitarian perception
of divine activity which is central to Niebuhr's
transformationist stance.

This completes Niebuhr's argument for the intelligibility of response analysis in the modern world.
Man-the-answerer adequately accounts for what we know

about the sociality, temporality, and contingency of self-existence. But it remains to be seen how this image adequately illumines a distinctly Christian understanding of human life. This question, which highlights the requirement of integrity, defines the task of Niebuhr's final chapter.

Under the influence of Paul's letter to the Romans, Christians tend to read scripture and the story of our life in light of the legal metaphor.[108] Sin and evil are understood as the results of past disobedience to God's law. This original disobedience spurs an inner conflict, since the self remains aware of divine law even as it follows another code. Guilt is one consequence, while the ultimate result of sin should also be construed legally as punishment.[109] "Salvation is the justification of the transgressor, his acquittal before the universal court despite his guilt."[110]

Though much illuminating thought about our life in sin and salvation has been developed along these lines, the legal image offers an inadequate interpretation of law and gospel. Gospel freedom becomes life lived under the higher law of love. But to love in obedience to commandment is not to love at all. The legal image transmutes the polarity of law and gospel into a paradox, since "it is required that one love unrequiredly."[111] Also, loyalty to God is an act of one's own freedom, but also an act of obedience to God's will. These and other dilemmas, says Niebuhr, "raise the question of the adequacy of the grand hypothesis, namely, that our life as agents in sin and salvation is fundamentally that of men-under-law or of obedience."[112]

In light of man-the-maker, sin is interpreted as missing the mark (hamartia), a vice which indicates perverse direction toward improper ends.[113] Disorder appears as conflict between this corrupt orientation and the proper telos of human life. Like original unlawfulness, this conflict originates with the genesis of self-knowing existence, though the fall is understood more as yielding to the temptation to be like God than as disobedience to divine command. The consequence of sin is a confusion in the face of contradictory drives and impulses which obscures the true good. Salvation becomes the restoration of the vision of God and the renewal of God's image in humanity.[114] Redemption restores harmony by reorienting the self toward its proper end and thus renewing its ability to pursue perfection.

The integrity of this scheme is questionable on two counts. First, the paradox of the vision and the image results in practical confusion about the true good or the true source of "oughtness" in Christian life. The goal of life is both the objective vision and the subjective perfection of the seer. But these different ends may come into conflict. There are important differences between the actions of a self committed to the transcendent good and the actions of a self in pursuit of spiritual perfection, as the example of otherworldly monasticism shows.

Second, teleology confuses the relation between human action and divine agency. Man-the-maker directs attention toward the human pursuit of the good. Descriptions of God and humanity as co-workers, co-makers, and co-creators result. But it is difficult to reconcile this emphasis with

the Christian conviction and experience of the primacy of God's action: in making himself known by the revelation of his goodness rather than allowing himself to be found by search; in giving the faith, the love, and the hope that aspire toward him; in creating and re-creating, making and remaking.[115]

Often, Christians try to combine these two approaches. But continuing debates over biblical interpretation, Pelagianism, legalism, and practical tasks of ministry indicate the inability of either theory to give unified insight into our existence in sin and salvation.[116] Responsibility, says Niebuhr, avoids the inadequacies of deontology and teleology while it accommodates their insights. In light of man-the-answerer, obedience and the pursuit of ideals are both responses, and there are other forms of response besides these two.[117] Response analysis recognizes the priority of divine action while it allows purposive activity as the appropriate response to God's directing action. Obedience remains an appropriate response to God's commanding action, but the fitting reply to gospel, as the declaration of divine forgiveness, is confidence in and loyalty to the One who values and saves.

From this perspective, sin may be understood as the loss of integrity demanded by or implicit in self-existence.[118] Disorder and conflict arise because selves respond in disunified and disparate ways to the diverse agencies that surround them. The self in sin is a polytheist who reacts to forces in various domains

160

by making disconnected responses. In responsiveness to the many, therefore, the sinful self is unresponsive to the One beyond the many.[119]

Conflict is raised to the pitch of self-contradiction, since the image of God as "a haunting sense of unity and of universal responsibility" remains even as the agent dissolves itself into a polyphrenic collection of moral patterns. To stay this struggle, the self is tempted to turn from the world's plural agencies back upon itself or its closed society. This henotheistic tendency provides unity, but of the most parochial kind.

In this state, the many powers and systems in the world appear to be arranged against the isolated self or isolated community. To the extent that people discern a single power or intention in the many, this one appears as the enemy or slayer. The appropriate response seems to be regard for self and survival. Defensiveness enters into all of our responses.

Salvation now appears to us as deliverance from that deep distrust of the One in all the many that causes us to interpret everything that happens as issuing ultimately from animosity or as happening in the realm of destruction.[120]

Redemption is the liberty to reinterpret the many agencies and powers in the world as contained within a total activity which destroys only to re-establish and renew. God's self-revelation enables us to redescribe all that happens, to construct a vision of all things appropriately related to the God who acts.

For Niebuhr, Christ enables this reinterpretation and the metanoia of our practical responses. As the man who responded to the One in all the many as friend, he is the incarnation of radical faith and universal responsibility. He is the paradigm and example of life lived appropriately in relation to God and to companions. As the person to whom God responded with renewal and resurrection, Christ is the one who elicits the conversion of people from distrust and misinterpretation to the liberty of confident and loyal reinterpretation. He is the "rosetta stone" or revelatory image in light of which we may begin the work of reconstructing our vision of our ultimate environment and readjusting our responses to it.

161

The structure of Niebuhr's argument for the integrity of response analysis parallels his previous arguments for its intelligibility. Man-the-maker and man-the-citizen illumine aspects of our life in sin and salvation. But the teleological image confuses moral life and leads to a portrait of the nature of human agency which threatens the priority of grace. The deontological image confuses the atonement and leads to an inadequate interpretation of the relation between law and gospel. By contrast, man-the-answerer avoids these difficulties and also offers a unified vision of self-existence in sin and salvation which is adequate to the perspective of radical faith and to a transformationist resolution of the basic theological categories.

This, then, is the conclusion of Niebuhr's essay in Christian moral philosophy. Both the integrity and the intelligibility of Christian ethics suffer when the classical symbols of teleology and deontology hold sway. An interpretation of Christian ethics that is intelligible in modern culture and has integrity to the biblical ethos can be worked in light of the metaphor of responsibility which emerges only in the modern world. This conclusion fits a wider maxim suggested as early as The Kingdom of God in America. Stating the faith intelligibly, so that it engages ordinary reason and experience, is a requirement for maintaining the integrity of Christian faith. Stating the faith with integrity, so that it adequately accounts for biblical patterns of divine action, is a requirement for maintaining the intelligibility of Christian believing.

[1]RS, p. 45.

[2]RM, pp. 11-16.

[3]Ibid., p. 11.

[4]Ibid., p. 21.

[5]Ibid., p. 16.

[6]Ibid., pp. 13, 22.

[7]Ibid., pp. 34-35; "Value Theory and Theology," pp. 111, 116.

[8]RM, pp. 25, 30-31, 33-34, 42, 48. For Niebuhr, the important issues of our time reflect the conflict of faiths. See H. Richard Niebuhr, "The Christian Church in the World's Crisis," Christianity and Society 6 (Summer 1941): 14.

[9]RM, p. 25.

[10]Ibid., p. 26.

[11]Ibid., p. 27.

[12]Ibid., pp. 27-28. See also CAW, p. 130 and "The Irreligion of Communist and Capitalist," pp. 1306-1307.

[13]RM, p. 28.

[14]Ibid., p. 29.

[15]Ibid., p. 32.

[16]For Niebuhr, this affirmation is consistent with Augustine's classical vision. See RM, 37; CC, 210; RS, 26.

[17]H. Richard Niebuhr, "Introduction to Biblical Ethics," Christian Ethics: Sources of the Living Tradition, ed. Waldo Beach and H. Richard Niebuhr, pp. 34-35.

[18]RM, p. 34.

[19]Jürgen Moltmann, The Crucified God, trans. R.A.

Wilson and John Bowden (New York: Harper and Row, 1974), p. 215. Daniel Day Williams' judgment that this is a biblical statement is closer to Niebuhr's intention. See Daniel Day Williams, The Spirit and the Forms of Love (New York: Harper and Row, 1968), p. 26. For Niebuhr, the identification of God with the source of all created being is also central to Augustine's theology. See H. Richard Niebuhr, "St. Augustine," Christian Ethics: Sources of the Living Tradition, ed. Waldo Beach, and H. Richard Niebuhr, p. 104.

[20] RM, pp. 32-33.

[21] Ibid., pp. 33, 44-48.

[22] Ibid., p. 47.

[23] Ibid., p. 48.

[24] Ibid., p. 45.

[25] Ibid.

[26] Ibid., p. 33.

[27] Ibid., pp. 46-47.

[28] Ibid., p. 47.

[29] Ibid., p. 40.

[30] Ibid.

[31] Ibid., p. 42; "Introduction to Biblical Ethics," Christian Ethics: Sources of the Living Tradition, ed. Waldo Beach and H. Richard Niebuhr, pp. 32-33, 35-36.

[32] RM, p. 42.

[33] Ibid., pp. 42-43.

[34] Niebuhr understands revelation primarily as the actions of God by which he makes his presence known to people, or as God's self-disclosure. He regards reasoning in faith on the basis of this revelation as a procedure in line with Augustinian theology. MR, pp. 104-114; "Revelation," Encyclopedia of Religion, ed. Vergilius Ferm, pp. 660-661.

[35] RM, p. 53.

[36]Ibid., pp. 55-56.

[37]Ibid., p. 58.

[38]Niebuhr refers to "the henotheism of the Son" in "The Doctrine of the Trinity and the Unity of the Church," p. 379.

[39]RM, pp. 61-63.

[40]Ibid., pp. 62-63.

[41]Ibid., p. 66.

[42]Ibid., p. 69.

[43]Ibid., p. 66.

[44]Ibid., p. 72. Compare Niebuhr's discussion here with his remarks about the principles of Christian constitutionalism, the independence of the church, and the limitation of power in KGA, pp. 59-87.

[45]RM, p. 73.

[46]Ibid., pp. 74-75.

[47]Ibid., p. 75.

[48]Ibid.

[49]Ibid., pp. 75-76.

[50]Compare this with Niebuhr's remarks about scientific method in "Value Theory and Theology," pp. 97-101.

[51]RM, pp. 86-87.

[52]Ibid., p. 88.

[53]Ibid.

[54]RS, pp. 45, 150.

[55]Ibid., p. 158.

[56]Ibid., p. 46.

[57]Ibid., pp. 45-46.

[58] Ibid., pp. 43-45.

[59] Ibid., pp. 65-67, 127-145.

[60] Ibid., p. 42.

[61] Ibid., p. 48.

[62] Ibid., p. 44.

[63] Ibid., p. 60.

[64] Ibid., p. 52.

[65] Ibid.

[66] Ibid., p. 60.

[67] Ibid., pp. 55-56.

[68] Ibid., p. 48.

[69] Ibid., p. 56. The responsibility metaphor emerges early in Niebuhr's writings. In "The Christian Church and the World's Crisis," p. 12, he asserts that religious faith affirms "a life of continuous responsibility."

[70] RS, pp. 57-58.

[71] Ibid., p. 60.

[72] Ibid., p. 61.

[73] Ibid., p. 59.

[74] Ibid., p. 66.

[75] Ibid.

[76] Ibid., p. 67.

[77] According to Niebuhr, the differences between teleological and deontological methods in ethics are modified in Christian ethics by reference to God as both the good and the source of the right. H. Richard Niebuhr, "Ethics, Christian," Encyclopedia of Religion, ed. Vergilius Ferm, p. 259.

[78] RS, p. 69.

[79]Ibid., pp. 71-73.

[80]Buber expresses this insight almost poetically. "In the beginning is relation--as category of being, readiness, grasping form, mould for the soul; it is the a priori of relation, the inborn Thou." Martin Buber, I and Thou, trans. Ronald Gregor Smith (New York: Charles Scribner's Sons, 1958), p. 27. For Cooley, "self and society are twin-born, we know one as immediately as we know the other, and the notion of a separate and independent ego is an illusion." Charles Horton Cooley, Social Organization: A Study of the Larger Mind (New York: Charles Scribner's Sons, 1913), p. 5. Mead claims that the individual experiences himself only "from the particular standpoints of other individual members of the same group, or from the generalized standpoint of the social group as a whole to which it belongs." George Herbert Mead, Mind, Self and Society, ed. Charles W. Morris (Chicago: University of Chicago Press, 1972), p. 138. Sullivan redefines the concept of human personality in social terms. Harry Stack Sullivan, The Fusion of Psychiatry and Social Science, ed. Helen Swick Perry (New York: W.W. Norton and Company, 1971), pp. 67-73.

[81]RS, p. 73.

[82]Ibid., p. 84.

[83]Ibid., p. 75.

[84]Ibid., pp. 78-79.

[85]Ibid., p. 82.

[86]Ibid., pp. 84-89; H. Richard Niebuhr, "The Triad of Faith," Andover-Newton Bulletin 47 (October 1954): 6-10.

[87]RS, p. 84.

[88]Ibid., p. 85.

[89]"The Triad of Faith," pp. 8-9. Though Niebuhr does not explicitly metion a transcendent reference group here, he does recall Nathaniel Taylor's statement "Let's follow the truth even if it leads over Niagara." It is not far fetched to count Taylor a member of a transcendent reference group which points beyond itself toward truth and embodies loyalty to that cause.

[90] RS, pp. 86-87; "The Triad of Faith," pp. 9-10.

[91] RS, p. 86.

[92] Ibid., p. 87. In "The Christian Church and the World's Crisis," p. 12, Niebuhr notes that "every religion supplies . . . a context, and the meaning and effect of the actions of its devotees is determined by the context."

[93] RS, pp. 87-88. As he did in Radical Monotheism, Niebuhr mentions a parallel between the pattern of universal response and the pattern of universal intent in scientific inquiry that is loyal to the cause of universal knowledge.

[94] RS, pp. 90-91.

[95] Ibid., pp. 91-92.

[96] Ibid., p. 92.

[97] Ibid., p. 94.

[98] Ibid., p. 98.

[99] Ibid.

[100] Ibid., p. 101.

[101] Ibid., p. 106.

[102] Ibid., p. 109.

[103] Ibid., pp. 111-112.

[104] Ibid., p. 121.

[105] Ibid., p. 117.

[106] Ibid., pp. 117-119.

[107] Ibid., p. 123.

[108] Ibid., pp. 127-128.

[109] Ibid., p. 128.

[110] Ibid., p. 130.

[111] Ibid., pp. 130-131.

[112]Ibid., p. 131.

[113]Ibid.

[114]Ibid., p. 133.

[115]Ibib., pp. 134-135.

[116]Ibid., p. 135.

[117]Ibid., p. 136.

[118]Ibid., p. 137.

[119]Ibid., pp. 137-138.

[120]Ibid., p. 142.

CHAPTER VII

A TRANSFORMATIONIST THEOLOGY IN THE PRESENT

Contemporary theology is distinguished by the bewildering variety of alternatives that have been proposed.[1] There are "death of God" theologies, theologies of story, liberation theologies, process theologies, theologies of hope, black theologies, feminist theologies, and revisionist theologies, to name a few. One thing is certain. All of them cannot be right.

Whatever the reasons for this pluralism, it demands that each responsible theologian articulate an explicit understanding of content and method.[2] What, in his or her view, are the main substantive issues to be resolved? What are the procedures that will help us resolve them? Also, it is imperative for the theologian to show that he is not just writing another book but has good reasons to believe that his proposal is more adequate than others. Accordingly, the broad objectives of this chapter are to state the understanding of content and method which follows from my analysis of Niebuhr's writings and to suggest why it is more adequate than at least some current alternatives.

At the level of content, my study has been chiefly concerned with the kind of language necessary to resolve the substantive issues. What is its logic? To what does it refer? At the level of method, I have been concerned with integrity and intelligibility as principles which check the adequacy of this language and the vision it articulates. What does it mean to say that a theology is true to the distinctive features of the biblical witness? What does it mean to say that it intelligibly engages the believer's contemporary life?

Language and Content

According to Niebuhr, theology is the disciplined development of reasoning in faith. Faith begins with a perception of God and proceeds toward the visible world.[3] Its reasoning applies revealed patterns taken to be disclosive of God and his purposes to the things and events of lived experience. This is a work of creative imagination. Believers interpret life in light of images cast up by distinctly religious experiences. They use the morphologies of special experiences to construe other experiences in relation to God, and this procedure gives the language of faith a literary and poetic quality as it reflects and raises questions in the midst of believing.

Faith's vernacular is symbolic because it begins with the remembrance of special events in the history of the believing community which point beyond themselves toward God and his purposes. Thus, the life, death, and resurrection of Jesus cast up images and elicit a faith commitment to the significance or value of God for human life. These special events, the images they suggest, and the sensibilities they evoke are beliefully realistic and lie at the basis of the Christian perspective.

As believers fit present experience with these interpretative keys, they arrange it in a beliefully realistic fashion from a Christian viewpoint. Experiences of ordinary life are construed theocentrically as mundane affairs which point beyond themselves toward God. In this way, interpretation helps to make the historic perception of the living Lord which gave rise to the religious images and sensibilities subjective and contemporary.

But interpretation does not take place in a vacuum. Believers interpret life in the context of a wider society which has already interpreted and understood experience on the basis of occasions, images, and sensibilities in its own history. When the believer applies distinctly Christian images to his experience, he applies them to experiences which have already been interpreted. This insight distinguishes Niebuhr's understanding of reasoning in faith from the estimates of more strictly confessional theologians.

The result of this interpretative process is not an original or first description but a redescription of the believer's experience. Facts, norms, beliefs, and circumstances which have already been interpreted are reinterpreted in light of beliefully realistic symbols and images. Since value itself is relational for Niebuhr, this reinterpretation alters the meaning or significance of things in the believer's ordinary experience by redescribing them in relation to God.

Niebuhr's articles about the Second World War exemplify this redescription. The believer experiences war, perhaps through the interpretative lenses of a nationalistic loyalty, as an interpreted fact of experience. In this context, the war is a struggle between

his country and its enemies. But he also apprehends
broad similarities between this fact of present experience and a distinctly biblical image in light of a
generalization about divine activity. Viewed in light
of the pattern of God's judging actions, this war is
like a crucifixion.

There are few hard and fast rules for the apprehension of this interpretative analogy. In light of
a pattern of divine activity expressed in the Bible,
creative imagination selects an image from the constellation of symbols cast up by revelation as its guiding
lens for reinterpretation. Nevertheless, as Niebuhr
construes the war with the aid of the cross, it becomes
apparent that the crucifixion illumines the meaning of
present experience. In light of this image, the common
events of the war are redescribed to highlight the
earnestness of self-sacrifice. The believer's attention is directed to the suffering of the guiltless as
a self-giving sacrifice and a call to repent from attitudes and actions of nationalistic pride and moralistic
retribution. The facts of the war have been redescribed, and they take on a new meaning and significance. As self-sacrifice and call to repentance, the
war is symbolic. It points beyond itself toward God's
present action and his purposes.

For Niebuhr, as for biblical theologians in-
spired by the theology of Karl Barth, faith's imaginative redescription of lived experience suggests that
God acts in and through particular historical circum-
stances.4 Theology is the disciplined development of
this suggestion. It seeks a pattern of divine activity
which discloses the morphology of divine action in all
events.

The constructive development of faith's suggestion involves at least three main steps: the inference of substantive categories of divine action,
their consistent resolution, and the redescription of
human experience. Substantive categories or principles
of divine action must be inferred from faith's redescriptive language, so that beyond reinterpretations
of particular experiences, theology can suggest a comprehensive vision of all things appropriately related
to God. The general categories of theology, then, are
abstractions from faith's imaginative speech about divine actions which share something of its symbolic
quality and enable a more general reinterpretation of
the world.

It is one thing to say that the images of crucifixion and judgment redescribe the meaning of the war
as an event in which God is at work. It is a related
but different thing to say that revelation transforms
our reasoned interpretations of the world. It is one
thing to say that crucifixion discloses God's action
in the tragic sacrifices of innocent people during the
war. It is another, if also related thing, to say that
God's goodness works in and through the tragedies of
sin and evil. The second statement in each pair is a
theological inference based, at least in part, on the
first, more concrete affirmation of reasoning faith.

Theology attends to the language of faith in
order to understand God's relation to the world. Interestingly, the theologian who does not participate
in the life of faith will find this inferential task
especially difficult, if not ultimately perplexing.
Though he has the same arsenal of biblical, historical,
and descriptive studies about the Christian community
available to him, he will find it more difficult to
distinguish faith's genuine and spurious expressions.5

For Niebuhr, at least ten general categories
arranged in polar relations emerge from this inferential process. They are reason and revelation, sin or
evil and goodness, law and gospel, nature and grace,
and church and world.6 Since Niebuhr did not write a
systematic theology, it is difficult to claim that
this list is exhaustive even for his own reflections.
Nevertheless, why one might settle on these five polar
relations can be indicated by a series of questions
which believers are likely to ponder as they try to
interpret the world theocentrically.

The categories remain symbolic because each
polar relation refers to an area of the believer's experience to God. Reason and revelation define an epistemological question. If I believe that special knowledge of God has been conveyed to me, how is this knowledge related to other things that I know? Sin or evil
and goodness raise the question of theodicy. If I believe that there is one God who is good and sovereign,
how can I understand the fact that there is sin and
evil in the world? Again, if I believe that the sovereign and good God is related to the sin and evil in the
world, it seems natural for me to ask whether faith in
this God has anything to do with the way I ought to
live. This is the question of moral value or "oughtness" in the Christian life signalled by law and
gospel.

Perhaps the most comprehensive work of believing imagination is required by the question of the Trinity posed by the relation between nature and grace. If I believe that the one sovereign God is related to good and evil, and also to the way I should live, then I may be prompted to ask how he is related to everything else in nature, culture, and history. Finally, the polarity of the church and the world raises the question of how the community loyal to God of which I am a member is related to others. If all this about God and his relation to evil and good, morality and nature be true for me and my companions, what is our relationship to those for whom it evidently is not true?

Christians have wrestled with these questions through the ages. They represent "problems which do not yield in years or even generations but require the devoted study of the Christian community for centuries."[7] Indeed, the terms of the questions and the questions themselves recur. They seem to follow psychologically, if not also logically, from belief in the one, good, and sovereign God made known through Jesus Christ.

My claim, then, is that relations between reason and revelation, sin or evil and goodness, law and gospel, nature and grace, and church and world define the main substantive issues for constructive theology. Once these issues have been identified, a second task of theology is to resolve them in a consistent manner. Indeed, a coherent understanding of the main substantive issues and their inter-relations forms a general hypothesis or construing belief about the morphology of divine action at the level of explicitly theological discourse. This construing belief forms the basis for a specific theological perspective that can be used to redescribe the general features of human existence in relation to God.[8]

Each of Niebuhr's types in Christ and Culture is a stance that adjudicates these substantive polarities in a consistent way and supports a major construing belief about God's action in the world. Thus, "against culture" Christians understand revelation as a deposit of special knowledge separate from the accumulated wisdom of culture, sin as a virulent disease which infects fallen society but exempts the holy community, morality as a set of laws for the life of the saints, and the Trinity in a way that qualifies God's creative and sustaining involvement in culture. The

church is set against and separate from the world.
This way of resolving the polar categories expresses
a major construing belief that informs theological construction: namely, that God reveals himself exclusively
in the life and teachings of Jesus and that to follow
Christ is to reject the claims of culture.

The radical's construing belief requires a
theological language which expresses the believer's
sense of separation from the world. Similarly, an "of
culture" stance requires a theological language able to
express the believer's sense that God is bringing the
best features of the world to fulfillment. For Niebuhr,
however, the project of construing the world theologically, or the task of faith seeking understanding, is
set in a transformationist key. His main construing
belief is that God is at work in all things reconciling
this sinful world to himself. What is required is a
language that expresses this sense of a world in the
midst of transformation, or a redescription of the
meaning and significance of all things in relation to
the totality of God's reconciling activity.

In order to redescribe the world, one must
either construct or choose a coherent interpretation
of human experience. Here, the theologian is on equal
footing with the believer. Both participate in cultural descriptions of ordinary experiences, and both try
to better understand the import of faith in God through
a redescription of already described experience. But
it is a task of the theologian to make this redescriptive process explicit. He must choose or fashion a
general interpretation of experience, show how it adequately interprets the theological categories, how it
adequately interprets human experience in light of common sense and also more disciplined contemporary knowledge, and show how experience interpreted in this way
may be coherently redescribed in light of his interpretation of the theological categories.

This distinguishes Niebuhr's theology from
Barth's attempt to understand Christian life exclusively in light of christological and biblical symbols. 9

The situation of Christians then seems to be
this: they cannot understand themselves or direct their actions or give form to their conduct without the use of the symbol Jesus Christ,
but with the aid of that symbol only they never
succeed in understanding themselves and their
values or in giving shape to their conduct.10

176

Since he employs general symbols as well as christological and biblical images, Niebuhr's theology is "Bible-
informed" rather than "Bible-centered."[11]

The task of interpreting human experience is
imaginative and symbolic. What is needed is a synec-
doche or root metaphor, an experience common to people
in our culture that sheds light on "the final circumambiency" in which we live and move.[12] The theologian,
therefore, takes a part of experience as symbolic of
the whole. "He pitches upon some area of commonsense
fact" and tries to illumine other areas of experience
in terms of this one.[13]

But western culture is a veritable fund of images which might serve as root metaphors. Niebuhr himself mentions images of the republic, the machine, the
mathematical system, and the organism.[14] It would be
easy to add others. For this reason, the theologian is
required, informally if not in print, to sift through a
vast collection. Of each one, he must ask whether it
promises an adequate interpretation of the theological
categories and human experience, with no prior assurance
that one will be found which satisfies these dual criteria. Since the choice of a root metaphor depends
partly on one's understanding of the substantive categories, and since it is quite possible that more than
one will be found adequate to significant features of
contemporary life, there is reason to expect a legitimate plurality of theologies. But the uncritical mul-
tiplication of inadequate metaphors can only contribute
to a chaotic proliferation.

In The Responsible Self, Niebuhr identifies
three major symbols that people have used to interpret
themselves, their values, their circumstances, and
their conduct. From his transformationist perspective,
he argues that man-the-maker and man-the-citizen are
not adequate theologically. They are not as intelligible to what is known about social, historical, and
religious features of human experience as man-the-
answerer, nor do they interpret the theological categories with as much integrity to the biblical witness.

In light of the metaphor of responsibility,
"the final circumambiency" of human life may be interpreted as a vast configuration of relations in which
people respond to the multiplicity of natural, historical, and social actions which impinge upon them. God
is the One beyond these many powers and agencies who
acts in and through the responsive relations of our

ultimate environment. Theology becomes reflection on the action and nature of God and the human response to that action and nature.15

Niebuhr's trinitarian doctrine of God may be interpreted as a pattern of divine activity to which people are called to respond that redescribes the responsive relations of our final circumambiency.16 To say that God is Creator is to redescribe that action by which we and our environment exist. It is to reinterpret this action, which has already been interpreted as the accidental conspiracy of a vast multiplicity of natural and historical forces, as the purposeful action of the good and sovereign God. At the same time, it is to commit oneself to respond to this action in ways that appropriately reflect its meaning and significance in relation to God. To say that this God is also Sustainer and Judge is to redescribe the actions of our environment which impinge upon us. It is to reinterpret these actions, which have already been interpreted as the actions of disparate agencies and systems in nature and history, as the ordering activity of the One who creates. Again, it is also to commit oneself to respond to this fabric of ordering activity which limits, sustains, and directs human possibilities in ways appropriate to its belonging to God. Finally, to say that God is Redeemer is to redescribe the ultimate action in our environment that destroys all things. It is to reinterpret this action, which has already been interpreted as the ontological law by which the self and all it prizes come to nothing, as "an intention and total activity that includes death within the dominion of life, that destroys only to re-establish and renew."17 It is to readjust our responses to all things in accordance with the awareness that this is the final purposive action of the One beyond the many.

For Niebuhr, this theocentric redescription of our ultimate environment is enabled by the life, death, resurrection, and reign in power of Jesus Christ. Through him, "we have been led and are being led to metanoia, to the reinterpretation of all our interpretations of life and death."18 The Christian life is one of appropriate response to the God who acts in and through sin and evil to bring about good, who enables and requires moral life, and who is related to all phenomena in nature and history. It is responsive life fitted to the theocentric context of universal life-giving action made known through the radical faith incarnate in Jesus Christ.

178

At this point, and really not before, the logic and referent of Niebuhr's properly theological discourse becomes fully apparent. The logic of theology, like the logic of faith, is imaginative and symbolic, though it operates at a higher level of generality. Theology reinterprets an imaginative interpretation of human experience in light of patterns of divine activity. The resultant vision of the world, its orders and tendencies, refers all things appropriately to God. Indeed, theological discourse is doubly imaginative since it expresses a symbolic interpretation of human experience that has been redescribed with the aid of imaginative patterns of divine activity.

Theological doctrines refer to this imaginative vision. They have a dual referent since they refer to ordinary experience interpreted in light of the metaphor of responsibility and then redescribed in light of patterns of divine activity informed by a consistent resolution of the substantive polarities. For this reason, doctrines cannot be reduced either to a simple repetition of the biblical witness or to a mere appropriation of other forms of discourse present in culture.

Principles of Method

This dual referent has important implications for integrity and intelligibility as principles of method. Integrity requires that a theological perspective be adequate to a revelation which transforms the believer's vision of the world. An adequate theology refers to biblical symbols as the informing basis for a redescription of experience in relation to God. Biblical symbols control theological construction in two ways. First, an appropriate root metaphor for the interpretation of human experience must be shown to be adequate to theological categories or principles inferred from faith's application of biblical images to lived experience. Second, an appropriate interpretation of human experience on the basis of an adequate root metaphor must itself be re-ordered or redescribed in light of biblical patterns of divine activity.

This is the force of Niebuhr's insistence that there is no valid knowledge of God prior to religious experience and his argument for the necessity of revelation in theology.[19] In a "Bible-informed" theology, there must be an irreducible reference to biblical images and symbols at the basis of its perspective. In order to construe human experience theocentrically, it is not enough simply to repeat the biblical symbols. But it is also inadequate to say that these images are simply translated into a contemporary idiom. Rather, the theological enterprise requires the active use of these symbols both in constructing and redescribing an adequate interpretation of human experience.

Where biblical images do not constitute the informing basis of a theological perspective or where the informing images of a theology violate or misrepresent faith's biblical expressions, the entire project of faith seeking understanding is skewed. The price paid for a lack of integrity is discontinuity with the disclosure of God to the biblical communities. There is little reason to think that a theology which lacks integrity will construe human experience in a way that points toward the same transcendent reality apprehended by the biblical communities. Indeed, if one believes that the living Lord of our present is the same active God disclosed in and through the biblical witness, then a theology which dispenses with or skews the biblical symbols jeopardizes its usefulness as an aid for discerning what God is doing in our present.

Intelligibility means adequacy to what is known about what is going on in light of contemporary knowledge and the ability to construe that from a Christian perspective. In short, it means adequacy to the believer's transformed experience of the world in relation to God. Niebuhr's transformationism does not call for a correlation of traditional Christian experience of God and contemporary experience as though these were two discrete sources for theological reflection.[20]

> Rather what one finds in the life of the
> Biblical people is what one finds in the life
> of faith in the present . . . to be aware of
> God's action upon us is also to be informed
> by God's action on Biblical events.[21]

The meaning and truth of human experience which theology must take into account is the meaning and truth of experience redescribed in light of paradigmatic, biblical images of divine activity.

The difference between a transformed vision of the world and other descriptions is a difference of perspective. Disagreement may reflect the use of different root metaphors for the interpretation of experience, the use of different symbols and images in the redescription of interpreted experience, or both. In either case, valid descriptions of the same feature of experience may differ, but they cannot be incompatible in the way that opposing claims as to whether or not a given feature is present are incompatible.

Thus, for example, a theological doctrine of regeneration must refer to what is known about human agents through modern modes of inquiry, e.g., philosophy and social sciences. It should be fashioned in light of biblical symbols in a way that is not incompatible with what else is known about human behavior. This, of course, does not mean that the doctrine of regeneration is reducible to concepts and categories which are not theological. The significance or meaning of certain features of experience and their impact on human existence is at issue here, and that remains open to differing interpretations. But it does mean that a theological reinterpretation and an accepted non-theological description of the same feature of experience cannot be incompatible in the way that opposing claims as to whether or not certain factors influence human behavior are incompatible.

Clearly, a transformationist understanding of intelligibility requires a specific understanding of the cognitive status of theological doctrines. To say that doctrines are redescriptive is to say that they refer both to judgments about what is the case (is-claims) and to judgments about the significance or meaning of what is the case (ought-claims). Doctrines depend in part upon factual evidence or what is presently known about what is the case, and this is more than an arbitrary relation. At the same time, redescriptive claims about meaning or significance are not simply derived from or entailed by factual claims about what is the case. In important respects, they are independent of factual claims and involve fundamental philosophical and theological considerations about the relationship between being and value.

In Niebuhr's theology, the relationship between being and value is expressed by his trinitarian apprehension of God. To identify the Creator with the Redeemer is to say that God is the source and center of being and value. The relationship between being and value is more than arbitrary because the Creator is also the Redeemer and because God's creative activity is neither separate from nor contradicted by his redeeming action. Redeeming grace is not discontinuous with created nature. On the other hand, value is not wholly determined by being since redemption is not simply the continuous development of created nature. Grace transforms nature. Value is related to being but does not inhere in it. To interpret human experience in relation to this apprehension of God is to make judgments about the meaning and significance of human experience or to redescribe it in the sense already indicated.

It is possible to argue that practical activity requires a vision which goes beyond judgments about what is the case. Persons are agents or responders who pursue and create possibilities as well as knowers who describe what they see. As responsive agents deciding among alternative courses of action, they need criteria and standards which are related to the way things now are but which are also drawn from the way things should be. For Niebuhr, this need for a source and center of meaning is the structural need for deity, and nothing less than a redescription of what is in relation to a center of value fulfills it.

What is required of the theologian is that he show that the facts as known are susceptible to a theological interpretation that does not distort them, and that such a theological interpretation goes beyond those facts to do justice to certain features of experience in a way that mere phenomenological description can never achieve. 22

This brings us back to the claim that theological doctrines cannot deny facts about human existence and the world that are generally accepted, even though they interpret the meaning and significance of these facts in a distinct perspective. But this is a problematical requirement since accepted facts about human existence and the world change through time. My claim, then, is that no matter what century people live in, the doctrines of theology must be intelligible to the way people understand themselves and their environment. There is no escaping historical conditioning in theological and non-theological knowledge.

A second problem is that the claims of experts about the facts sometimes disagree. Thus, some psychological interpretations, e.g., Freud, have been rejected on grounds that they are incompatible with theological redescription. At this point, recourse is taken to the fact that experts in the field of psychology disagree. Again, it sometimes happens that the experts agree and are wrong, e.g., Ptolemy.23 Nevertheless, it remains the case that the theologian's redescription cannot deny what the theologian knows and affirms on non-theological grounds without landing squarely on the horns of double truth.

These few observations lead to an interesting, if also potentially discouraging, conclusion. The possibility of a transformationist vision depends on some measure of agreement about the facts of human existence and the world as well as some malleability or looseness with respect to the interpretation of their significance. Where no appreciable agreement exists, or there is no appreciable openness about the significance of what is known, human experience cannot be coherently redescribed. There may be times and societies in which what is known and affirmed on non-theological grounds actually precludes the possibility of a transformationist vision. Perhaps the scientific system of eighteenth-century Europe is a case in point. It may have been too closed to accommodate a transformationist redescription. To admit this possibility, at least, is to affirm that humans are fated to inquiry within the bounds of important social and historical limitations.

An intelligible theological redescription of the world is continually in conversation with valid, non-theological accounts offered by other accepted areas of inquiry. This conversation enriches Christian faith and theology, but it also presents profound and enduring difficulties. For Niebuhr, no greater challenge confronts theology than to display the meaning and import of Christian faith in relation to fundamental quests of the human spirit.24

Current Alternatives

To my knowledge, no one on the contemporary scene has written a comprehensive statement of Christian doctrine in accordance with the understanding of content and method I have just described.25   If this estimate is accurate, if Niebuhr's typology in Christ and Culture is reliable, and if my analysis of his theology holds, then it follows that the transformationist alternative of Augustine, Calvin, Maurice and others is presently absent as a systematic option.

It is, of course, one thing to say that a venerable conception of theology has been neglected and quite another to claim that this neglected conception is more adequate than the present field of options. Validation of the latter claim would require an

exhaustive account of contemporary theologies. I have
settled on the more modest course of suggesting good
reasons to believe that a transformationist theology is
more adequate than others through an analysis of two
current alternatives: namely, the writings of Paul
Holmer and Schubert Ogden.

To choose these two from the chaotic plurality
of present options is somewhat arbitrary. However, the
heuristic distinctions in Christ and Culture can be
used to illumine Holmer's theology as a "paradox" position and Ogden's as an "above" position. My aspiration
here is to use these two examples to show that the
transformationist option is more adequate. The obvious
implication is that the transformationist position is
more coherent in the modern world than either the
paradox or above positions as disclosed in Niebuhr's
analysis.

For Paul Holmer, fidelity to faith's experience, adequacy to the Bible, and adequacy to reason require that theology be radically distinct and even separate from knowledge gained through other inquiries.26
God's love "fixes a chasm between Godliness and worldliness, between believers and unbelievers."27 Faith's
experience involves a conversion of spirit that affects
the inward passions of the human heart.28

Scripture, says Holmer, is the record of the
convictions, passions, beliefs, and God-centeredness of
early evangelists, apostles, and believers which fits
a distinctive form of life.29 As God's word, it addresses our "dearly bought expectations and wishes."30
It is a "divine magisterium" that remains the same
from age to age and instructs Christians in the art
of living.

Theology is an interpretation with two foci
which mediates between "the varying passions of men and
the abiding verities of God."31 Though he proposes
something eternal, the theologian must also study "the
particular concerns and pathos of the day" in order to
articulate God's truth in "the common diction of jeal-
ousy, fear, love, repentance, hate and anxiety, of
which we are masters already."32 So conceived, theology is interpretation in a constricted sense.33 It
does not keep up with changing beliefs current in the
world, but instead strives toward the simplicity of a
vernacular which touches the passions and refers its
hearers to a Christian life-context.

One of the recurrent reasons for the unclarity
of the language of learned people is the very
process by which they try to effect accommoda-
tions between ethico-religious concepts and
language, on the one side, and scientific
concepts and language on the other.[34]

Vague metaviews about the historical development of
doctrine come to grief over the fact that appropriately
constricted theological interpretation is not affected
by either change or increment in our non-theological
knowledge about human existence and the world.[35]

This constricted enterprise is intelligible for
Holmer because all that can be gotten from any interpretative tongue is an interpretation adequate to a
specific and discrete context of life and logic. The
logic and context of scientific discourse is not the
same as the logic and context of religious discourse.
Indeed, there are no meaningful connections between the
two. "Each has its context, its occasion, its own
province, and its own function, relative to a specific
need."[36] The fact that a scientific explanation and a
theological one are "incommensurable" betrays no logical incompatibility.[37] The language of religion, or
theology, is an intimate, radically personalistic and
confessional expression of the religious life.[38] Passion is its context.[39] By contrast, scientific discourse is disinterested, detached and neutral language
about language. It is about ethics or about aesthetics
or about love or about religion.

Scientific language about religion (as well as
almost anything else) and religious language
(which I have called theology--an expression
of religious passion dominated by religious
categories) do lack those factors which would
allow the first to confirm the second, either
to contradict the other, or either to replace
the other.[40]

Thus, what is true of scripture theologically
has no necessary relation to what is true about it in
non-theological terms. What is true of human life and
the world theologically has no necessary relation to
what is true about human life and the world in non-
theological terms. "Rationality is polymorphic."[41]

Without disputing the specific achievements of
science and scholarship in the least, it still
remains true that there is another cosmos to

185

which every person has an immediate access; and
this cosmos is the inner and personal life and
the locus of moral and religious pathos . . .
But it is nonetheless true that moral and religious judgments are, in turn, about everything
else in the world--about, in short, the large
cosmos in addition to ourselves and God.42

Though Holmer lapses into uncharacteristic unclarity
himself at this point, he clearly wishes to maintain
that faith's passionate and personalistic speech makes
judgments about all else in the world. Paradoxically,
these judgments about the large cosmos have nothing
whatever to do with other judgments and interpretations
about the same thing.

     To his credit, Holmer criticizes theologies
which too readily translate distinctly Christian categories for interpretation into non-theological terms.
To his credit also, he has suggested a general interpretation of language and meaning which is compatible
with his highly constricted notion of theology, though
the logical status of this general interpretation is
somewhat puzzling.43 He insists that theologies which
do not strive for the simplicity of a common diction
that engages the varying passions of the heart "are actually changing their subject."44 In order to be true
to scripture, theology must do today what it has done
in the past for a Paul or a James. If it does not intelligibly engage the passions of the heart, it loses
its integrity to the divine magisterium.

     Nevertheless, the astounding claim that this
highly constricted language of theology bears no necessary relation to scientific discourse about anything is
unacceptable from a transformationist perspective. It
is plainly incompatible with our understanding of intelligibility and the affirmation that doctrines depend
in part on what is presently known in non-theological
quarters about what is the case. But this methodological difference is just the tip of an iceberg.

     From a transformationist viewpoint, Holmer's
position is unacceptable on philosophical, religious,
and methodological grounds. It is philosophically unsatisfactory because it denies the historically conditioned nature of theological interpretation. Of
course, Holmer might protest that this denial is itself
based on philosophical grounds which separate theological interpretations from changes in non-theological
inquiries. But the ready response to this rejoinder is

that Holmer's Wittgensteinian analysis of language, truth and logic is the historically conditioned product of a particular age and place. A Holmerian interpretation of doctrine is itself partly dependent on a particular philosophy. And, though it proves to be an unusual interpretation, it is quite compatible with the "vague metaview" that Christian doctrine develops historically in relation to non-theological knowledge.

Holmer's position is religiously unsatisfactory because it implies a deficient understanding of the Trinity. The chasm that divides theological interpretation from other forms of discourse also threatens to drive a wedge between God the Creator and God the Redeemer. To claim that the special knowledge of God conveyed to our passional nature cannot be effectively related to the other things we know about human nature and the world is to fail to take theological account of a significant part of God's creation. A genuinely trinitarian theology tries to construe all things in nature and history theocentrically. It regards the disinterested enterprise of science as a feature of the natural and historical world to be interpreted in light of God and his purposes. To isolate theological discourse about human existence and the world from developments in non-theological knowledge about human existence and the world is to frustrate faith's conviction that the perception of the sovereign Lord is relevant to all areas of life. Precisely because Holmer isolates theological discourse from important areas of human experience in the modern world, he fails to construe all of life in relation to God.

Finally, Holmer's stance is methodologically inadequate because it fails to meet the standards of both intelligibility and integrity. To say that what is true about human life and the world theologically has no necessary relation to what is true about human life and the world from other perspectives is to affirm a doctrine of double and, perhaps, multiple truth. Though Holmer admits this consequence in a remarkably forthright manner, the fact remains that double truth presents formidable difficulties for the believer.

Granted that theological interpretations of the crucifixion are not reducible to the terms of historical reconstruction, is a given theological interpretation compatible with <u>any</u> historical account which might be accepted as true? If on historical grounds it could be shown that Jesus of Nazareth was not crucified, would this have any bearing on a theological interpretation

187

of his passion? If one accepts claims of sociologists
and psychologists about the formation of human personality, does this have any bearing on theological understandings of regeneration, sanctification, and moral
responsibility?

For Holmer, believers and theologians must
simply be trained to think about these and other matters in light of his polymorphic doctrine of truth.
But there is good reason to think that they will find
that tutelage more confusing than illuminating in matters of religious life and belief. There is also good
reason to think that they ought to resist it.

Difficulties with the intelligibility of
Holmer's position lead, eventually, to severe problems
of integrity. One wonders how Holmer can affirm that
religious expressions which were adequate and meaningful in the past carry the same meaning in the present,
alongside his claim that all theological interpretation
refers primarily to inner and personal life. Do biblical expressions about God's ordering, sustaining, and
redeeming power, about God's acts of judgment, about
the life and ministry of Jesus Christ, about the end-
time, and about moral requirements carry the same meaning when their significance is thought to be exhausted
by their reference to one kind of truth among others,
and when the one kind of truth to which they refer is
primarily and even exclusively an inward, personal
truth of passion? Or, is it the case, as the transformationist is obliged to think, that what began
as an effort to preserve the meaning of faith's past
expressions has ended by changing their content?

For Schubert Ogden, who tends toward Niebuhr's
synthetic type, the theologian must discover a conceptuality "in which he can appropriately state what faith
itself affirms and, at the same time, so express its
affirmations that they can be clearly understood" by
contemporary hearers.[45] In this, he follows Rudolf
Bultmann. One task of theology is to translate the
mythical and symbolic utterances of faith into the literal terms of an appropriate idiom.[46] The task of con-
ceptualizing the faith makes the theologian "gratefully,
though not uncritically" dependent on philosophy.[47] It
requires "nothing less than that 'right' philosophy
which is the essential prerequisite of any adequate
theological construction."[48] Choosing the right philosophy is a critical work to be undertaken in light of
the affirmations of Christian faith and the basic
realities of our experience.

188

Not surprisingly, Ogden believes that one difficulty with much recent theology is its failure to be
sufficiently critical in its choice of the right philosophy. This is true even of so accomplished a theologian as Rudolf Bultmann. Heidegger's existential philosophy is too "anthropologically one-sided." [49] Though
it provides a strong analysis of possibilities for
human self-understanding, it fails to provide an adequate conceptuality for talking about God and his
action.[50]

Precisely at this point, says Ogden, Charles
Hartshorne's dipolar theism makes a significant contribution, because it presents an understanding of God
which corresponds to Heidegger's understanding of
man.[51] Hartshorne explicates "the structure of the
divine action" and makes clear "that God in his very
being is a God who acts."[52] In short, "The 'right'
philosophy for Christian theology is not Heidegger's
analysis of man alone, but his analysis in conjunction
with Hartshorne's dipolar doctrine of God."[53] A careful melding of these two promises a theology which
explicates the authentic possibilities for human
existence in relation to God presented by Christian
believing.

Ogden skillfully argues for the adequacy of
this approach in his essay on "The Reality of God."
The contemporary theologian, he says, is confronted
with an apparently insoluble dilemma. On the one hand,
the classical theism which has accompanied much theolo-
gizing in the West conceives of God as an entirely ac-
tualized being. Metaphysically, which is to say really,
the divine being is immobile and at rest. Autonomous
and free human action can have no true significance for
the supremely diffident One of classical theism and is,
therefore, ultimately meaningless. On the other hand,
this difficulty is exacerbated by a secularistic outlook which not only affirms human autonomy, but also
denies the meaningfulness of all statements about non-
empirical realities on the grounds that empirical
methods define the limits of human cognition. Apparently, one must either affirm classical theism and
deny human autonomy, or affirm autonomy and deny the
reality of God.

For Ogden, however, the dilemma is false. The
theologian is under no compulsion to adopt either classical theism or modern secularism. The former fails to
interpret symbolic and mythic expressions in the Bible
about divine activity. These expressions can be true

189

only virtually or metaphorically for a theology which borrows its conceptuality from classical metaphysics and defines God as perfection at rest. Thus, classical theism either eliminates these expressions altogether or reduces them to the status of primitive legends.[54]

Secularism presents an incoherent account of human experience in both its cognitive and practical dimensions. It is epistemologically incoherent since, whether stated in verificationist or falsificationist form, the dictum that valid knowledge must be empirical is itself empirically unverifiable. A true analysis of cognition, says Ogden, shows that empirical methods have limits which, in Kantian fashion, point toward a non-empirical, transcendent ground. Statements about God are therefore quite compatible with the autonomous pursuit of scientific knowledge.[55]

The practical incoherence of secularism can be demonstrated by a similar analysis of secularistic morality. Atheistic existentialists try to found morality on the belief that autonomous human action is the only thing of unconditional significance. But this attempt leads them to proclaim the unrelieved absurdity of human life, since autonomous man on his own no longer has any assurance that the world is receptive to human action or that moral life is worthwhile. Camus' Sisyphus and rat-infested city express it best. While autonomous moral life never achieves its appropriate ends, the only authentic thing for people to do is to affirm the meaningfulness and worthwhileness of human autonomy by investing moral action with unconditional significance in spite of this fact. Anything less than the recognition that autonomous moral life is for naught is fundamentally dishonest. Anything less than authentic existence in the face of this recognition denies the proper significance of human freedom.

For Ogden, this portrait of moral life is incoherent, since it fails to provide any reason to be moral or authentic, just as the empiricist dogma fails to provide any reason to believe in the worthwhileness of scientific inquiry.[56] The point is that our confidence in the worthwhileness of autonomous inquiry and autonomous moral life requires a fundamental reassurance which secularism cannot provide. The secularistic outlook, which begins by affirming the exclusive meaningfulness of autonomous life, ends by failing to support meaningful activity of any kind. To the extent that the actions of modern people continue to presuppose the worthwhileness of autonomy in its cognitive and practical dimensions, they do not really believe humanity is on its own. The actions of modern people proclaim that the limits of autonomous moral life, like those of scientific inquiry, point toward a transcendent ground.

This leads Ogden to affirm that the secular faith in autonomy which necessarily accompanies modern science is coherent, while its degenerate secularistic forms are not. Legitimate secularity affirms the meaningfulness of autonmous morality as well as autonomous inquiry. But it does not insist, as does secularism, that all valid knowledge is necessarily empirical or that humanity is simply on its own. If secularity is valid, however, then it delivers a cogent critique of classical theism. Traditional theism must be recognized as a particular "cast of thought" which has lost its usefulness in the modern period.[57]

Fortunately, Hartshorne's dipolar theism is able to express faith in the God who acts in a way that is not only compatible with modern secularity, but forms its unavoidable presupposition. Unlike the older theistic scheme, the neo-classical metaphysic envisions God as a dynamic being actualizing his existence in response to his creatures. In response to the actions of creatures, God actualizes himself differently than would have been the case if those creatures had not acted as they did. The free, autonomous actions of people have an unconditional significance since they have some genuine effect on the actualization of the supreme being whose existence is absolute and eternal.[58] Moreover, because God conceived in this way acts in history by "luring" his creatures on toward the actualization of appropriate possibilities, divine action may also be conceived in a way that respects the freedom of human agents.[59]

Thus, for Ogden, the neo-classical metaphysic reinforces the confidence secular people need to lead autonomous lives, because it assures them that ultimate reality respects their freedom and is receptive to their autonomous action. This dynamic conception of God is also true to the biblical witness, since it offers adequate interpretations of the very myths and symbols of divine action which the classical theism threatens to eliminate from meaningful theological discourse. From Ogden's perspective, then,

modern secular man, with his characteristic

191

affirmation of our life in the world in its
proper autonomy and significance, is in a
peculiarly good position to discover the
reality of God--nay, has already made that
discovery at least implicitly. 60

In fact, when the myths, symbols and affirmations of
Christian faith are properly translated, it becomes
apparent that they express the fundamental faith in
the worthwhileness of human existence that is characteristic of secularity. Christianity re-presents the
basic existential faith which modern people share in
some degree as the condition for the possibility of
their lives as autonomous selves. It answers the existential question concerning the meaning of human life
which modern secularity presents as the question of
freedom or autonomy.61

The distinction between secularity and secularism shows that Ogden is more critical of the cultural
Zeitgeist than are many radical theologians.62 His
criticisms of Bultmann show that he exercises greater
care in his choice of the "right" philosophy than do
many other theologians, and he legitimately criticizes
actus purus as a concept of God which is inadequate to
biblical portraits of divine activity and to meaningful
affirmations of human agency.63 Nevertheless, Ogden's
translation of biblical symbols into the conceptuality
of Hartshorne's dipolar theism involves an unsatisfactory interpretation of human experience that leads to
an inadequate conception of divine activity.

For Ogden as for Hartshorne, the dominant concept is "creative synthesis."64 This principle emerges
from "the way in which one interprets or experiences
the world," the way one thinks and feels his environ-
ment.65 The vast multiplicity of influences molding
our experience flow together to produce a single unity, namely, the experience of the moment. But there
is a causally unbridgeable gap between the many and
the one. "An emergent synthesis is needed, to decide
just how each item is to blend into a single complex
sensory-emotional-intellectual whole, the experience."66 This creative synthesis becomes the model
for human freedom.

When this concept is generalized as the ultimate principle of reality, the structure of divine action must also be conceived as an instance, though the
eminent one, of creative synthesis. God is conceived
to act in such a way as to contribute to the creativity

192

of all creatures. This is not the result of a divine choice or self-limitation, but an alleged necessity of the metaphysical position. God "intends the fullest possible self-realization of each of his creatures and infallibly acts to do all that can be done to that end."67

There are subtle differences between Hartshorne's concept of creative synthesis and Niebuhr's metaphor of responsibility. Though both account for the subject's interpretation of the environment, Niebuhr's metaphor is more closely bound to an analysis of practical action. While Niebuhr affirms that our experiences involve interpretations and that our responses are connected with these interpretations, he does not assert that all our practical responses are creative. At least some of the things to which we respond cut "athwart our purposive movements."68 They represent "the denial from beyond ourselves of our movement toward self-realization or toward the actualization of our potentialities."69

For Niebuhr, our experiences of suffering have this character. Paul Ricoeur's more recent analysis of the will seems to express something of Niebuhr's insight. There are certain conditions and events to which we can only consent, and our responsive consent does not look forward to a new possibility for our self-actualization engendered by our willingness to conform to the condition or event in question.70 Can we meaningfully speak of practical creativity in our response to these conditions and events? To consent to the fact of these conditions changes my disposition toward them. But it does not change the fact that my movement toward creative self-actualization has been cut off. Does the rubric of creative synthesis or free response or optimizing possibilities fit the phenomenon of consent as well as Niebuhr's metaphor of responsibility?

The answer to this question is crucial because, if it can be said that some elements in our ordinary experience thwart our creativity (but not our capacity to act), then it will be possible to conceive of divine actions which intend something other than the fullest possible self-realization of people and do something other than contribute to the creativity of all creatures. In short, it will be possible to achieve something other than an anthropocentric conception of God, or one that infallibly supports legitimate human interests and values.

From a transformationist perspective, Ogden's use of Hartshorne's dipolar theism reduces to a species of utilitarian Christianity in which God can do nothing other than support human self-fulfillment. But this amounts to a misreading of both the order of nature and divine action. It is inadequate to disjunctions of human experience and also to important mythic and symbolic expressions of divine action in scripture. The difference between Ogden's synthesis and Niebuhr's transformation runs deep. The fundamental issue is a different estimate of the biblical witness and the texture of human experience.

Though Ogden rejects the uncritical manner in which some liberals of the nineteenth century adopted the predominant cultural outlook, his own theology seems open to a similar criticism. Following his critique of secularism, we expect him to show how central affirmations of Christian faith judge and transcend secularity as well. Otherwise, it appears that Christianity has nothing distinctive to say to the world. But the key principle of creative synthesis prevents this, and demands that Ogden's process theology re-present secular confidence in the meaningfulness of human creativity rather than transform or redescribe it.

These inadequacies of Ogden's theology emerge at the level of content in his understanding of sin or evil and goodness. It is essential to the process metaphysic that God "lure" his creatures on to good.71 It would seem to follow, then, that this divine effort to persuade recalcitrant humans to realize the good by presenting authentic possibilities is all God can do and all that needs to be done about evil in the world.72

For Ogden, then, God's eternal trying, his eternally responsive attempt to persuade people to actualize creatively appropriate possibilities, is enough to vouchsafe the final victory over sin and evil.73 But this is only to restate the implicit belief of the process metaphysic that the human exercise of free creativity and the divine intention finally correspond, that sin neither radically penetrates creative human wills nor holds them firmly in bondage. For the possibility that some people in the exercise of their creative freedom will reject this persuasion, as it appears many do, is never regarded as a serious threat.

Nevertheless, the biblical witness starkly admits this possibility and even admits that, on the basis of our present experience, there is little reason to hope that the tragedy of sin and evil will be overcome. As Van Harvey points out, it is precisely at this point that the Bible and much traditional Christian theology call on a power of God that is something more than merely persuasive, and does something more than optimize the fullest possible expressions of human self-realization.[74] And it is exactly this sort of power which the process view must deny or reduce to the status of primitive legend.

But this means that the Bible, including its accounts of Jesus' life, ministry, and death, is hardly uniform in the affirmation that human life as we know it is worthwhile. To the degree that the New Testament writers and Jesus himself apparently look forward to an action of God that will judge this world and bring in his kingdom, one might argue that they are able to assure us of the meaning of this life only through a radical hope for its divine transformation. In short, Christian faith appears to provide a more profound assurance than the low-level reassurance required to keep the machinery of autonomous action in working order. Far from merely re-presenting secular confidence in human creativity, this more profound assurance actually judges and transforms it.

No doubt, some will object that this transformationist resolution of the theodicy problem reinstates the "existential repugnance" of classical theism, since it calls for divine activity which thwarts human creativity. The implication is that transformationism harbors an inadequate doctrine of the Trinity, since the Redeemer destroys the creative freedom with which he has endowed his creatures.[75] But, in light of the phenomenon of consent and the aspects in which human will is involuntarily determined, Hartshorne's interpretation of the nature of human agency is questionable. It seems possible to interpret the created human capacity to act under the rubric of responsibility, and to claim that this capacity to act is not destroyed by divine actions which thwart human creativity.

Another objection to our transformtionist interpretation is that it admits serious inconsistencies in the Christian vision. Why should a good God with this kind of power allow sin and evil in the first place, much less let it continue?

195

This is not the place to detail the distinction between the good for humanity in isolation and the true good of the universal community of which God is a part which would inform a full answer to this question.[76] There are many conditions and events which are only apparently evil from the perspective of isolated human purposes. Of course, even after this has been said, it must also be admitted that there are ethically irrational evils in the world. The transformationist will insist that the biblical estimate of this ethical irrationality requires that adequacy to experience take priority at this juncture over logical consistency. He will also insist that the persistent and all too contemporary experience of that same ethical irrationality, to which writers like Sartre and Camus testify, points toward the same conclusion. Contemporary and biblical accounts of the experience of evil, juxtaposed with the biblical and also human hope for something better, require a theology bold enough to make this admission. The traditional problem of evil is more than a pseudo-problem.[77]

At the level of method, Ogden's theology fails to meet the standard of integrity. The synthesis of Christian faith with the conceptuality of process philosophy fails, since Hartshorne's concept of creative synthesis and his dipolar structure of divine activity cannot support the literal translation of biblical expressions which Ogden sets out to accomplish. The result is a theology which suffers a loss of important elements in the religious heritage, since a theology which accommodates God's actions to human self-actualization finally misconstrues the God of the Bible.

These difficulties lead also to problems of intelligibility. Ogden's portrait of human creativity fundamentally undespairing of and undisturbed by the ethical irrationalities of the world neglects important aspects of our modern experience. To demonstrate Camus' inconsistency misses the point. Human experience in the modern world is something less than logically self-consistent, and secular confidence in human autonomy is more profoundly threatened than Ogden's analysis allows. Not only does the same irrationality of evil perceived by the biblical communities infect and threaten our present, but we have to deal in our present with the same God who inspires fear and trembling among biblical witnesses even as he works for reconciliation. Ogden's proposal, which begins as an effort to conceptualize divine activity in a way that engages the basic realities of our experience, ends by misrepresenting the God who acts and denying important features of contemporary life.

To summarize, Holmer's "paradox" position implies a deficient understanding of the Trinity, inappropriately reduces biblical expressions about divine activity to truths of passion, and fails to construe modern scientific knowledge in relation to God. Ogden's "above" position implies a less than radical doctrine of sin, inappropriately reduces biblical expressions of divine activity to actions which infallibly facilitate human self-realization, and denies the profound threat to secular life posed by the ethical irrationality of the world. Thus, it would appear that neither the paradox nor the above positions described in Christ and Culture is optimally coherent in the modern world.

Constructive Theology

These remarks suggest some important points about constructive theology. For Niebuhr, dual loyalties to Christ and culture define the theological task. At the level of content, these loyalties are reflected by five substantive polarities: reason and revelation, sin or evil and goodness, law and gospel, nature and grace, and church and world. The stance that a theologian takes on any one of these relations must be consistent with the stances he takes on any one of the others. Otherwise, his interpretation of doctrine will be informed by an inconsistent belief about God's activity in the world and will lapse into incoherence.

A coherent interpretation of doctrine becomes intellectually possible when a symbol or metaphor provides a comprehensive interpretation of human experience which is informed by a stance on each of the polar issues as well as by contemporary knowledge. Presumably, some theologians will work with a metaphor and move toward a resolution of the polar issues, while others will begin with the polar issues and emerge with a dominant metaphor.78

At the level of method, dual loyalties to Christ and culture are reflected in the principles of integrity and intelligibility. The question of method is whether a substantive theological perspective is adequate both to the modern world and to the distinctive features of the biblical witness. However, content is prior to method since different conceptions of these

197

principles emerge from alternate resolutions of the polar relations.

Once a substantive interpretation has been accomplished, the stance on the polar relations, the metaphor, and particular articulations of specific doctrines may be tested in light of the methodological principles. Though this procedure is admittedly circular, it allows the theologian to display and critically review his principal judgments about subject matter and method to check whether they are coherent and adequate. Thus, method may be influential in determining content since integrity and intelligibility determine the adequacy of substantive interpretations.

The transformationist theologian who follows this program cannot simply repeat Niebuhr's theology. At the level of content, nothing less than a systematic statement of Christian doctrines is needed to demonstrate the adequacy and coherence of a transformationist approach. Such a statement requires that one identify the central doctrines of Christian theology. It will go beyond Niebuhr's own work to construct a full-scale treatment of those doctrines in light of the metaphor of responsibility and a transformationist resolution of the substantive polarities. At the level of method, where Niebuhr's comments are few, this systematic treatment will require an explicit statement of procedures that meet criteria of integrity and intelligibility, if it is to be apprehended critically and fulfilled rationally.

It seems appropriate, at this point, to recall Niebuhr's insistence that "no mediating theology in history has ever been able to keep in balance the opposing elements it seeks to reconcile."[79] A transformationist theology faces considerable tensions between its dual loyalties at the levels of content and method. Perhaps these tensions cannot be harmoniously resolved, though to present Christian faith with integrity and intelligibility is an enduring and compelling responsibility.

Notes

[1] Gordon D. Kaufman, _An Essay on Theological Method_, American Academy of Religion Studies in Religion, no. 11 (Missoula, Montana: Scholars Press, 1975, pp. ix-x.

[2] David Tracy, _Blessed Rage for Order: The New Pluralism in Theology_ (New York: Seabury Press, A Crossroad Book, 1975), p. 3.

[3] RM, p. 14.

[4] "War as the Judgment of God," pp. 630-633; "Is God in the War?" pp. 953-955; "War as Crucifixion," pp. 513-515; MR, pp. 34, 111; "Introduction to Biblical Ethics," _Christian Ethics: Sources of the Living Tradition_, ed. Waldo Beach and H. Richard Niebuhr, p. 22; RS, pp. 126, 136-137; James M. Gustafson, _Theology and Christian Ethics_ (Philadelphia: United Church Press, A Pilgrim Press Book, 1974), pp. 135-136.

[5] RM, pp. 12, 15.

[6] That the polarity of church and world should be included seems to follow from Niebuhr's remarks in _The Purpose of Church and Its Ministry_ (New York: Harper and Row, Harper's Minister's Paperback Library, 1977), pp. 25-27. The types in _Christ and Culture_ may be grouped according to conceptions of the church. Also, the relation between church and world forms an important concern for Niebuhr during the thirties and forties.

[7] H. Richard Niebuhr, Daniel Day Williams and James M. Gustafson, _The Advancement of Theological Education_ (New York: Harper and Brothers, 1957), p. 74.

[8] The notion of a "construing belief" comes from Julian N. Hartt, _The Restless Quest_, pp. 89-90. For Hartt, a construing belief involves an intention to draw inferences and to "see" or view things in relation to it. In a sense, Christian faith is a worldview. See Julian N. Hartt, _Theological Method and Imagination_, p. 15. My point is that theology, as faith seeking understanding, is the attempt to construe all things in light of Christian faith in God, to construct a worldview, to redescribe all things in relation to God in light of a construing belief.

[9] RS, p. 158.

[10] Ibid.

[11] Ibid., p. 46.

[12] Ibid., pp. 52, 153, 160.

[13] Stephen C. Pepper, World Hypotheses: A Study in Evidence (Berkeley, California: University of California Press, 1942), p. 91. Niebuhr refers to Pepper's work in RS, p. 153.

[14] RS, p. 153; "John Calvin," Christian Ethics: Sources of the Living Tradition, ed. Waldo Beach and H. Richard Niebuhr, p. 271.

[15] James M. Gustafson, "Introduction" to H. Richard Niebuhr, The Responsible Self, p. 40; "Introduction to Biblical Ethics," Christian Ethics: Sources of the Living Tradition, ed. Waldo Beach and H. Richard Niebuhr, p. 22.

[16] The trinitarian pattern of Niebuhr's theology is discussed by James M. Gustafson, "Introduction" to H. Richard Niebuhr, The Responsible Self, pp. 2-32. It is also indicated by our discussion of the transformationist stance in Christ and Culture, and in our discussion of The Kingdom of God in America. In our discussion of Radical Monotheism, we noted that Niebuhr's description of God as the center and source of being and value, which guides his interpretation of culture, is an abstract statement of the confession that God is Creator and Redeemer.

[17] RS, p. 142.

[18] Ibid., p. 143.

[19] "Value Theory and Theology," p. 116; MR, pp. 30-31.

[20] See David Tracy, "Particular Questions Within General Consensus," Consensus in Theology? A Dialogue with Hans Kung and Edward Schillebeeckx, ed. Leonard Swidler (Philadelphia: Westminster Press, 1980), pp. 33-34.

[21] James M. Gustafson, "Introduction" to H. Richard Niebuhr, The Responsible Self, p. 28.

[22] Gordon D. Kaufman, God the Problem (Cambridge, Massachusetts: Harvard University Press, 1972), p. 33.

[23]Stephen Toulmin and June Goodfield, The Fabric of the Heavens: The Development of Astronomy and Dynamics (New York: Harper and Row, Harper Torchbooks, 1961), pp. 115-127.

[24]H. Richard Niebuhr, Daniel Day Williams, James M. Gustafson, The Advancement of Theological Education, pp. 76-77.

[25]Gordon Kaufman's Systematic Theology: A Historicist Perspective comes closest. Julian Hartt's work also seems to be informed by a similar understanding of theology, as does the work of James M. Gustafson.

[26]Holmer's position is most clearly stated in two essays, "What Theology Is and Does," and "Scientific Language and the Study of Religion." The latter appeared originally in Journal for the Scientific Study of Religion 1 (October 1961): 42-55. Both are published in The Grammar of Faith.

[27]Paul Holmer, The Grammar of Faith, pp. 8, 76.

[28]Ibid., pp. 16, 19, 36; Paul Holmer, Theology and the Scientific Study of Religion, The Lutheran Studies Series, vol. 2 (Minneapolis: T. S. Denison and Company, 1961), p. 18.

[29]Paul Holmer, The Grammar of Faith, pp. 8, 76.

[30]Ibid., p. 14.

[31]Ibid., p. 16.

[32]Ibid., p. 16.

[33]Ibid., pp. 14-15.

[34]Ibid., pp. 74-75.

[35]Ibid., p. 3.

[36]Ibid., p. 69.

[37]Ibid.

[38]Ibid., pp. 62-63.

[39]Ibid., p. 74.

[40]Ibid.

[41]Ibid.

[42]Ibid., pp. 72-73.

[43]Ibid., pp. 111-135.

[44]Ibid., p. 16.

[45]Schubert M. Ogden, "Bultmann's Demythologizing and Hartshorne's Dipolar Theism," Process and Divinity: The Hartshorne Festschrift, ed. William L. Reese and Eugene Freman (LaSalle, Illinois: Open Court Publishing Company, 1964), p. 494.

[46]Schubert M. Ogden, The Reality of God, p. 117.

[47]Schubert M. Ogden, "Bultmann's Demythologizing and Hartshorne's Dipolar Theism," p. 493.

[48]Schubert M. Ogden, The Reality of God, p. 119.

[49]Schubert M. Ogden, "Bultmann's Demythologizing and Hartshorne's Dipolar Theism," p. 501.

[50]Ibid., pp. 498, 503.

[51]Ibid., pp. 505-506.

[52]Ibid., p. 508.

[53]Ibid., p. 511.

[54]Schubert M. Ogden, The Reality of God, pp. 49-52.

[55]Ibid., pp. 27-33.

[56]Ibid., pp. 27-42.

[57]Ibid., p. 19.

[58]Schubert M. Ogden, Faith and Freedom: Toward a Theology of Liberation (Nashville: Abingdon, 1979), pp. 79, 84-85.

[59]Ibid., pp. 76-77, 90-95. According to Ogden, God acts to "optimize" the freedom of his creatures for "possible self-actualization." See also Schubert Ogden, The Reality of God, p. 227.

[60]Schubert M. Ogden, The Reality of God, p. 44.

[61]Schubert M. Ogden, Faith and Freedom, pp. 46-47.

[62]Schubert M. Ogden, The Reality of God, pp. 14-15; David Tracy, Blessed Rage for Order, pp. 31-32.

[63]Schubert M. Ogden, The Reality of God, pp. 17-18.

[64]Schubert M. Ogden, Faith and Freedom, p. 75.

[65]Charles Hartshorne, Creative Synthesis and Philosophic Method (LaSalle, Illinois: Open Court Publishing Company, 1970), p. 5.

[66]Ibid., pp. 5-6.

[67]Schubert M. Ogden, Faith and Freedom, p. 90.

[68]RS, p. 60.

[69]Ibid.

[70]Paul Ricoeur, Freedom and Nature: The Voluntary and the Involuntary (Chicago: Northwestern University Press, 1966), pp. 344-345.

[71]Schubert M. Ogden, Faith and Freedom, p. 79.

[72]Ibid., p. 90; Van A. Harvey, "The Pathos of Liberal Theology," Journal of Religion 56 (October 1976): 382-391.

[73]Schubert M. Ogden, "Evil and Belief in God: The Distinctive Relevance of a 'Process Theology,'" Perkins Journal of Theology 31 (Summer 1978): 33.

[74]Van A. Harvey, "The Pathos of Liberal Theology," p. 390.

[75]This possible criticism recalls Niebuhr's assertion that the synthesist expresses better than others "the principle that the Creator and the Savior are one, or that whatever salvation means beyond creation it does not mean the destruction of the created." CC, p. 143.

[76]"Value Theory and Theology," pp. 109-110.

[77]Schubert M. Ogden, "Evil and Belief in God," p. 34.

[78] James M. Gustafson, Protestant and Roman Catholic Ethics: Prospects for Rapprochement (Chicago: University of Chicago Press, 1978), p. 155.

[79] KGA, p. 194.

APPENDIX

A NOTE ON THE LITERATURE

Niebuhr's transformationist perspective includes basic convictions, a distinct understanding of the content of theology, a coherent resolution of that content, and certain broad principles of method. Though the available literature about Niebuhr has some merits, it fails to grasp this unity. Consequently, his interpreters either analyze diverse features of his theology or try to develop it in ways that skew its integrity.

A number of the essays in Faith and Ethics: The Theology of H. Richard Niebuhr (1957) take motifs in Niebuhr's theology as their point of departure. Four undertake direct expositions of his thought. Hans Frei's essay on Niebuhr's theological background concentrates on nineteenth and twentieth century European theology, but ignores Niebuhr's stated indebtedness to Jonathan Edwards and the pragmatic tradition in America.[1] Though his essay on Niebuhr's theology identifies conversionism, valuation, relativism, the Trinity, and the person of Christ as major themes, it is not comprehensive, and Frei prematurely concludes that Niebuhr is closer to Barth than to Troeltsch.[2]

The conversionist motif is central in Paul Ramsey's article on "The Transformation of Ethics." Interestingly, Ramsey criticizes Niebuhr's penchant for relativism and the threat that it poses to the objectivity of values. He argues that Niebuhr's theory of values is more relational than relativistic and that both conversionism and radical monotheism can be affirmed without prejudice to the objectivity of moral norms. Only Niebuhr's philosophical conception of historical reason, a "lesson he learned (too well?) from Troeltsch," requires that large concessions be made to relativism at this point.[3]

George Schrader analyzes Niebuhr's relational theory of values on its philosophical merits, though he is aware that it has the theological consequence of guarding the goodness of God from determination by prior value judgments.[4] Unfortunately, Schrader's assumption that Niebuhr's theory is founded on the relation between existence and essence or the potential of individuals for self-actualization is incorrect and has disastrous theological implications from Niebuhr's viewpoint. Niebuhr himself rejects Schrader's interpretation and insists that his theory of values rests on the relation of self to others.[5]

The Promise of H. Richard Niebuhr by John Godsey (1970) is an introduction to some of Niebuhr's basic convictions rather than a critical analysis of his writings. Godsey packs a remarkable number of observations into his short text. He mentions Ernst Troeltsch as a continuing influence on Niebuhr's thought, records Niebuhr's ambivalence toward Barth's dogmatic theology, and acknowledges the influence of American Christianity on Niebuhr's affirmation of divine sovereignty.[6] He identifies the analysis of human faith, revelation in history, the sovereignty of God, sin, grace, conversionism, and the church as major themes in Niebuhr's theology.[7]

But Godsey makes no effort to trace the development of Niebuhr's thought in detail and believes that no attempt to systematize it can communicate its richness.[8] Not surprisingly, he closes with a rather loose list of questionable and promising elements in Niebuhr's theology. Questionable elements include Niebuhr's historical relativism, the orthodoxy of his trinitarianism and of his christology "from below."[9] Promising elements are Niebuhr's lack of defensiveness or his "non-apologetic confessionalism," his understanding of faith as trust and loyalty, and his uncompromisingly radical monotheism.[10]

Libertus A. Hoedemaker's The Theology of H. Richard Niebuhr (1970) is the first truly comprehensive interpretation of Niebuhr's theology. Hoedemaker's focus on the style of Niebuhr's thinking allows him to take a wide range of factors into account. He is careful to distinguish the American context for Niebuhr's reflections and also the influence of Jonathan Edwards.[11] He is sensitive to the importance of Niebuhr's liberal heritage in Europe and America. According to Hoedemaker, Troeltsch's influence is most apparent in Niebuhr's method of analyzing Christianity as a social entity and his occupation with the problem of compromise or cultural synthesis in The Social Sources of Denominationalism, The Kingdom of God in America, and Christ and Culture.[12] Hoedemaker is sensitive also to the influence of Karl Barth, though he seems ill at ease with Niebuhr's criticisms of Barth's theology.[13]

Though he regards transformation as a major theme, Hoedemaker never really comes to grips with the

typology in Christ and Culture or the distinctiveness
of Niebuhr's stance.14   His conclusion, that Niebuhr
presents a style of reflection more than a systematic
approach to the problems of theology, occasions another
list of prominent problems and convictions in Niebuhr's
thinking.   More seriously, it opens the door to
Hoedemaker's preoccupation with the "dynamic relation
between history and eschatology which is implied in
consistent attention to the missionary structure of
Christian faith."15   This angle of vision skews the integrity of Niebuhr's perspective.   It leads Hoedemaker
to qualify Niebuhr's trinitarian identification of God
with the principle of being, to break the connection
between God and the present order of reality, and to
suggest a moratorium on talk about God.16

To See The Kingdom: The Theological Vision of
H. Richard Niebuhr by James Fowler (1974) contains
a complete bibliography of Niebuhr's writings and is
the most detailed account of the inner development of
Niebuhr's thought.   Fowler's method is to interpret the
organism of Niebuhr's thinking through prominent metaphors and symbols.17   He believes that the dominant
symbolic patterns of Niebuhr's theology are essentially
in place by 1937.   There is truth to this judgment,
though one wonders whether the model of divine action
and human response emerges with clarity before the
forties.18   Fowler believes that Troeltsch provides
Niebuhr with an example of polar and typological thinking and that he also draws Niebuhr's attention to the
importance of valuation in theology.   Also, he notes
that Niebuhr offers a genuine alternative to Barthian
and liberal theologies.19

Fowler's attempt to take the reader inside
the dynamic of Niebuhr's thought neglects Christ and
Culture, and relies on unpublished manuscripts which
are unavailable for public scrutiny.   His conception of
Niebuhr's genuine alternative remains something of a
mystery.   Instead, the inherent looseness of Fowler's
approach leaves dangling allusions, e.g., the affinity
between the "Process-structural metaphor" in Niebuhr's
theology and Whiteheadian metaphysics.20   It also leads
Fowler to conclude with yet another list of Niebuhr's
strengths and weaknesses.

What was a dangling allusion in Fowler's book
is the principal thesis of Donald E. Fadner's The
Responsible God: The Christian Philosophy of H. Richard
Niebuhr (1974).   Fadner is concerned that Niebuhr's
sense of God and God's activity jeopardizes human

responsibility and believes that a consistent implementation of Niebuhr's philosophical theology leads in
the direction of process thought.21   He carefully describes the place of philosophy in Niebuhr's theology
and then argues that a resymbolization of God on the
model of the responsible self will make Niebuhr's
program more consistent.   The result is a portrait of
the responsible God who is partly dependent on his
creatures, presents man with the possibility of realizing eternal life, and cannot be implicated in the free,
evil assertions of human beings which do violence to
the body of God.22

        Perhaps this is the systematization of
Niebuhr's thought that so many interpreters fear.
Fadner himself is aware that his perspective involves
"a good deal of abstraction" from Niebuhr's writings
and personal development.23   Indeed, it does violence
to what we find there.   Behind Fadner's concern that
Niebuhr jeopardizes human responsibility is the assumption that secular autonomy must be affirmed.   But this
angle of vision overlooks significant differences between Niebuhr's metaphor of responsibility and secular
portraits of human freedom, while it neglects the
subtleties of Niebuhr's critique of the value theory
of American empirical theologies.24   For these reasons,
Fadner's implementation of Niebuhr's theology not only
obscures Niebuhr's own concentration on the God who
acts and renders his insistence on the initiative of
divine agency problematical, but it also introduces
elements foreign to Niebuhr's idea of human responsi-
bility.25   Surely, Niebuhr's God is dynamic, and he
has no intention of denying human responsibility as he
understands it; but Fadner's argument wrongly assumes
that the only way to affirm human agency and also have
a dynamic concept of God is to embrace the metaphysic
of process philosophy.

        Lonnie D. Kliever's H. Richard Niebuhr (1977)
analyzes main themes in Niebuhr's theology.   Kliever
correctly notes that theocentrism, historical relativism, and conversionism are major motifs in Niebuhr's
thought but fails to see that conversionism represents
a coherent resolution of the content of theology.   Perhaps this accounts for his refusal to develop the suggestion that Niebuhr's work has systematic implica-
tions.26   In any case, Kliever concludes with yet another review of Niebuhr's theological ambiguities and
a list of some themes in contemporary theology which
Niebuhr anticipates.   According to Kliever, ambiguities
include the relation between personal and impersonal

images in Niebuhr's conception of God, the validity of historically relative perspectives, and precisely what is changed by God's transformative action.[27] Niebuhr anticipates contemporary discussions about foundational or philosophical theology, the turn toward symbolic language and narrative in religious speech, and the problem of anthropocentric attitudes toward the environment.[28] The list is true as far as it goes but reflects confusion about the unity of Niebuhr's perspective and fails to bring his theology into serious dialogue with current alternatives.

In sum, the literature about Niebuhr is uneven. It contributes to our understanding of major themes in his theology but fails to grasp the unity of his thought and to provide a reliable interpretation of its relevance for the constructive task. There are also gaps in our understanding of the development of Niebuhr's thought. Given the fact that he wrote his dissertation on Troeltsch, that he mentions Troeltsch as an important influence in three of his major works, and that Troeltsch's distinctions repeatedly emerge in Niebuhr's writings, what seems necessary is a comprehensive study of Niebuhr and Troeltsch. It is also notable that there is no published study of Niebuhr's American theological background.

Notes

[1] Hans W. Frei, "Niebuhr's Theological Back-
ground," Faith and Ethics: The Theology of H. Richard
Niebuhr, ed. Paul Ramsey (New York: Harper and
Brothers, 1957), p. 10.

[2] Hans W. Frei, "The Theology of H. Richard
Niebuhr," Faith and Ethics: The Theology of H. Richard
Niebuhr, pp. 65-67, 92, 104-116.

[3] Paul Ramsey, "The Transformation of Ethics,"
Faith and Ethics: The Theology of H. Richard Niebuhr,
pp. 162-163.

[4] George Schrader, "Value and Valuation," Faith
and Ethics: The Theology of H. Richard Niebuhr, p. 204.

[5] RM, p. 105.

[6] John D. Godsey, The Promise of H. Richard
Niebuhr (Philadelphia: J. B. Lippincott Company, 1970),
pp. 14, 21, 41-43.

[7] Ibid., pp. 22-81.

[8] Ibid., p. 96.

[9] Ibid., pp. 101-102.

[10] Ibid., pp. 97-103, 110-113.

[11] Libertus A. Hoedemaker, The Theology of H.
Richard Niebuhr, pp. 1-7, 33-38.

[12] Ibid., p. 17.

[13] Ibid., pp. 26-27.

[14] Ibid., p. 45.

[15] Ibid., p. 163.

[16] Ibid., pp. 164-166.

[17] James W. Fowler, To See The Kingdom: The
Theological Vision of H. Richard Niebuhr, p. 249.

[18] Ibid., p. 253.

[19] Ibid., pp. 57-61, 256.

[20]Ibid., p. 251.

[21]Donald E. Fadner, The Responsible God: The Christian Philosophy of H. Richard Niebuhr, p. 230.

[22]Ibid., pp. 238-239.

[23]Ibid., pp. xiii-xiv.

[24]See chapter six of this dissertation and "Value Theory and Theology," pp. 95-96.

[25]See Gordon D. Kaufman, God The Problem, p. 128.

[26]Lonnie D. Kliever, H. Richard Niebuhr (Waco, Texas: Word Books, 1977), p. 175.

[27]Ibid., pp. 167-174.

[28]Ibid., pp. 180-189.